good-
enough
mother

good-enough mother

The Perfectly *Imperfect* Book of Parenting

René Syler
with Karen Moline

SIMON SPOTLIGHT ENTERTAINMENT
New York | London | Toronto | Sydney

SSE

SIMON SPOTLIGHT ENTERTAINMENT
An imprint of Simon & Schuster
1230 Avenue of the Americas, New York, New York 10020
Copyright © 2007 by René Syler
All rights reserved, including the right of
reproduction in whole or in part in any form.
SIMON SPOTLIGHT ENTERTAINMENT
and related logo are trademarks of Simon & Schuster, Inc.
Designed by Steve Kennedy
Manufactured in the United States of America
First Edition 10 9 8 7 6 5 4 3 2 1
Library of Congress Cataloging-in-Publication Data
Syler, René.
Good-enough mother : the perfectly imperfect book of parenting /
by René Syler with Karen Moline. — 1st ed.
p. cm.
ISBN-13: 978-1-4169-3491-2
ISBN-10: 1-4169-3491-X
1. Syler, René. 2. Mothers—United States—Biography.
3. Motherhood—United States. 4. Parenting—United States.
5. Perfectionism (Personality trait). I. Moline, Karen. II. Title.
HQ759.S96   2007
306.874'30973—dc22
[B]
2006102669

To Casey and Cole, the treasures of my heart

acknowledgments

I have so many people to thank, most of all my wonderful off-spring, Casey and Cole, without whom my life would be boring beyond belief. Sure, I'd sleep until noon every Saturday and maybe even have more sex with my husband, but hey, it's the price I pay.

I also need to thank Buff Parham, much to his chagrin: You are fantastically (bordering on fanatically) organized, and there are no words to describe how grateful I am for your belief that I can accomplish everything I set my sights on. Now stop picking up after me.

Because good-enough mothers existed in generations past, I have to thank my mother, Anne Syler. Forgive me for what I said in the book (you can't sue someone for telling the truth, and I am your daughter). My respect for you is immeasurable, and my love for you even more so.

To my kid sister, Tracy: What else can I say but thanks for living closer to Mom than I do? Kidding. Your wise counsel and steady shoulder have provided me with support over the years. I pray I'm not going to have to pay for that.

To the other fantastic Tracy in my life, Tracy Parham, who took over mommy duties while I endured a hellacious commute from Dallas to New York every week. Those kids are adorable from fifteen hundred miles away, aren't they? You were great as a stand-in mommy, and I can never repay you. I hope you don't ask.

To Jahayra Guzman, my work wife: I have no idea how you kept my life, the kids' schedules, and Buff's appointments straight and managed some semblance of a personal life yourself. Thank you for being the boss of me.

To Patrece Williams and Kim Serratore, my hair and makeup artists, who made me look so good not just for the cover of this book but each and every day on *The Early Show*. You two are talented beyond words and I miss you madly.

To my best good-enough mother, Stacey: Where would I be without you? Thank you for saving me seats at the school play year after year, and because of you, my kids have a fighting chance of getting book order money in on time. I appreciate the camaraderie, and thanks for not making me feel stupid when I do something that is, well, stupid.

To Mrs. Henry: I'm sorry, 'nuf said.

To Mr. McCullough: I told you I could be a success without math. Perhaps I'd have done better if you'd told me I'd need it to count my money. Or figure out what 30 percent off a pair of Jimmy Choos is. Come on, man, think real world!

To my crack publicist, Linda Lipman: You're an ace at what you do. Do you remember where *Good-Enough Mother* was conceived? In the backseat of a car on the way to New Jersey. You and I birthed it together. We'd better never break up, or someone's paying child support out the wazoo.

To Henry Reisch: You've been my TV agent as long as I've been married to Buff; thank you for guiding my career with your steady hand and talking me off more ledges than I can count.

To my literary agent, Mel Berger: Because of you and your calm demeanor, super-tough negotiating skills, and always-pithy e-mails, *Good-Enough Mother* found the right home with the right people.

To Deborah Feingold, who snapped a bunch of terrific photos of the kids and me: Nice job. Your shutter speed was fast enough to capture an eight-year-old boy flying around the studio in Heelys.

I have so many thank-yous for the folks at Simon Spotlight Entertainment. To Jennifer Robinson and Betsy DeJesu: Thanks for helping us get the word out about *Good-Enough Mother*. You have made countless women feel better about pizza for breakfast and pancakes for dinner. Who says carbs are bad?

To Michael Nagin, who designed an awesome cover with these photos: You did a phenomenal job of capturing the essence of *Good-Enough Mother*. I don't even look like I'm screaming on the inside.

To Jennifer Bergstrom: You were a girlfriend right from the moment we broke bread and shared salad and wine. Thank you for believing in me and my message, for making my life-long dream of being an author come to fruition, and, above all, for picking up the check at that hellaciously expensive place!

To my cowriter, Karen Moline: What else can I say except that you're amazing? Thank you for showing me the ropes and for your patience and (sometimes not so) gentle nudging. Your ability to take my words and make a book is truly a sign that you should have been paid more. I love you.

And finally, to my phenomenally talented editor, Patrick Price, who is not a mother (or even my gender), but who still unstintingly embraced my philosophy. Thank you for honing my words into something mothers everywhere will under-stand. You are an honorary good-enough mother.

contents

good-enough mother

introduction:
welcome to my world

IT'S ANOTHER BUCOLIC AFTERNOON AT THE Parham estate.

Note that I like to call it the Parham "estate," in honor of my married name, as that conjures an image of a white-gloved butler greeting me at the door, chilled martini on a silver tray. Don't be fooled. It's the whirlwind of C, C, and O that surrounds the car as soon as I pull up, with nary a glove in sight.

In the words of boxing announcer Michael Buffer: "Let's get ready to RUMBLE!"

For years, as one of the anchors on *The Early Show* on CBS, I needed to be up at three thirty a.m. so I could get ready and into our midtown Manhattan studio to be on-air at seven a.m., before staggering home at one p.m. C and C are the formidable team of Casey and Cole, my offspring. Olivia is our demented yellow Lab, sixty-eight pounds of pure jumping, chasing, drooling, and leather-chomping muscle. She's not huge but she's strong as a whip, and her grip on whatever garment she chooses to shred is strong enough to pull down a weeping willow. Today she has something in her mouth that I optimistically assume is one of the bones I boiled especially for her. Casey and Cole race past me to our backyard pool with a friend, and so I get a free moment to take a closer look at just what's in Olivia's grip.

No, it's *not* a bone—it's one of Cole's brand-new school shirts, which I just got from Kohl's. And now Olivia is drooling all over it as she puts more holes in the jersey!

"BAH!" I shout at Olivia while chasing after her like a madwoman.

See, I'm not supposed to say "Stop it!" or "I'll wring your neck!" thanks to Bark Busters. The theory behind Bark Busters is that you don't teach a dog English—you have to speak "dog." Hence the "BAH!" So when Olivia jumps on top of me when covered in mud, I say "BAH!" When she pees in the house, I cry "BAH!"

Not surprisingly, whenever I'm BAH-ing at her, my husband, Buff Parham, thinks I've lost what little mind I have left. Honest to God, I've started to worry that I'll damage my vocal cords because I'm BAH-ing so much at this dog.

Anyway, back to bucolic. There I am screaming "BAH!" at Olivia when I notice that the kids have seized a large green garbage bag from the kitchen and are now playing with it in the pool. Forgetting the strained vocal cords, I run screaming, hands waving, out to the pool deck.

"THAT IS SO DANGEROUS!" I shout at them. "CUT IT OUT RIGHT THIS MINUTE! PEOPLE SUFFOCATE LIKE THAT!"

What kind of mother am I? The kids could suffocate *and* drown. Great. I've given them not just one but two ways to die.

Welcome to my world!

And my husband wonders why I'm delirious at dinnertime. By the time he gets home, I'm no longer capable of having an adult conversation.

All I can manage is "BAH!"

But you know what? I don't beat myself up about it. I'm a good-enough mother, and that's the way it is. With all the insanity of my three-ring circus, I've learned that if one of the 3,412 balls I'm juggling drops, I just pick it up and start juggling again.

I'm a "path of least resistance" parent. When I was pregnant with Cole, and Casey was about two, I came home from a particularly grueling day at work. It was the kind of day that, if I hadn't been pregnant, would have ended with an overdose of carbs and cabernet. As I propped my sequoia-size ankles on the coffee table, Casey toddled in. Sure-footed in her Stride Rites, she proceeded to climb on top of the table, nearly breaking her neck right in front of me. She's always been an astute child, and I guess she innately knew that a woman who'd just worked twelve hours and who was carrying around thirty-five pounds of baby (oh, all right, *eight* pounds of baby—the rest was my padding) was not going to challenge a nimble two-year-old. Buff was no help at all. Although he wasn't pregnant, he also was in no mood to crack the whip. (Never mind that eight-and-a-half years later he *still* isn't in the mood.)

So go ahead, I thought as Casey teetered close to the brink of disaster. *I'm a good-enough mother. Right now my feet need to be up, and I know I'm just limber enough (for a pregnant and bloated water buffalo) to catch you if you fall.*

Much of my inspiration comes from my own mom. Yep, Anne Syler was the original good-enough mother. She was the first intimate example I had of a mother who worked outside of the home and kept things running with no outside help.

My kid sister, Tracy, and I grew up in Sacramento, California, right in the very middle of middle class. When all the other neighborhood kids' moms were at home, ours was at her job. It wasn't so much about the money—although we needed that, of course—but about my mother's need to stay engaged. She was the one who taught me that life is about full contact: suiting up every day, going out there and doing battle, coming home to make dinner, listening to your kids squabbling, and then getting up and doing it all over again.

Mom likes to tell the story of Tracy coming home from kindergarten one day. Still a stay-at-home mom then, Mom stood waiting for her at the corner, as usual. Tracy glanced up at her, and said, "Mom, what are you doing here? I wanted to walk home *all by myself*." Crushed, Mom went home and threw herself onto the bed, sobbing that she wasn't needed anymore. Then she picked herself up and found a job in a home for special-needs kids.

And then she adopted the "son" she'd never had, a crazy cockapoo we named Michael.

More important, she learned a critical lesson—that she had to live for *herself* as well as for her family. Ever since I'd been born, she had subsumed her own needs into those of her family's, taking care of me and my sister and our rather demanding father. It was time for Mom to reclaim her own identity.

I thought of Mom (and Michael) after a recent conversation with a former colleague who is now mom to two beautiful kids. She told me she needed my advice (gasp!) because in her mind I had always seemed to manage the home/work/children thing with aplomb (ha!). She was tearing herself to shreds because she had gotten stuck working late on Halloween and had missed taking her kids trick-or-treating.

"Ginger," I said to her. "First of all, you are doing the absolute best you can. And, quite frankly, your children are too young to know what trick-or-treating really is. So dress them up this weekend and hunt for candy in your backyard. They won't know the difference. Next year, when they're older, you can take them door-to-door."

I have a lot of friends and colleagues like Ginger: smart, accomplished women who are reduced to tears when they space a playdate. Or when they forget it's picture day at school and they let their son wear a shirt emblazoned with the words "I Do All My Own Stunts." (Okay, that was me.)

I'm not a parenting expert, but I am the mother of two great children, which gives me daily on-the-job good-enough-mother training. I've read loads of those parenting books cover to cover, and none of them talk to me about the realities of parenting a mini-me like my son, Cole. None of them show me how to deal with the real minutiae of daily living. Or what to do when my sensitive and rule-abiding daughter comes home sobbing from school one day because one of her best friends flagrantly flaunted school regulations by chewing gum on the bus. Or how to respond when my son comes running into my bedroom, claiming to be a new kind of superhero, with his jammie bottoms and briefs adorning his head, shrieking, "Mom! Mom! When I fart, underwear comes shooting out—because I'm UNDERWEAR MAN!"

Instead, these well-thumbed advice books make me feel woefully inadequate because Casey and Cole aren't always prone to doing what books suggest they should be doing. My children aren't perfect, and neither am I.

Okay, so it took me forty-four years to figure that out, but I *do* know what I'm doing most of the time—and I'm good enough at doing it.

So I've decided that we good-enough mothers need all the advice we can get, as long as it has nothing to do with feeling obliged to bake homemade cupcakes with hand-beaten buttercream frosting and topped with calligrapher's piped swirls of "Happy Birthday," and as long as it has *everything* to do with the realities of the stress and pressures in our lives in the twenty-first century.

The heart of my philosophy is not about giving kids less— but about giving today's stressed-out mothers *more*. Believe me when I say that this is not about the overplayed war between working moms and stay-at-home moms. In my mind, if you're a woman with children, you *are* a working mom!

And you know you're a good-enough mother when, like me, you have:

- bought something from the local grocery store, removed the plastic wrapping, and passed it off as your own at the school bake sale.
- used a stapler to hem your daughter's pants as she's walking out the door for school.
- sworn in front of the kids, only to hear that the words were taught to half the kids in day care the next day.
- realized that you haven't had a good night's sleep since the last baby was born because your mind is so busy with keeping your work and home life running smoothly, connecting with your kids' teachers, not missing the first day of gymnastics that you scheduled two months before,

managing your husband's schedule—all the while trying desperately to remember and retain some of the person you were before all these people came crashing into your life!

- blithely pushed the foregoing thoughts to the back of your mind because you've decided to take a weekend off by yourself because, frankly, your life does not and never will revolve around your kids' every single waking second, and sometimes you need to recharge your own batteries in order to keep the machinery of your family well oiled.

Good-enough mothers recognize that if they believe they *are* good enough, then they will be. You have to believe it to sell it. This pithy nugget of salesmanship came from years of on-the-job training; you can't report on things that you don't know. If you still believe, deep down, that you aren't good enough, then you'll never be able to convince your kids (and yourself) that you mean business.

And if you're a woman with a husband like mine, you're the only parent with a thumb firmly on the pulse of family life—keeper of all schedules, master arranger of playdates, chief homework helper, kisser of skinned knees, ace negotiator, booker of handymen, and all-around gofer girl.

In short, it's a big job but you're good enough to succeed.

Yep, a Good-Enough Mother is a real GEM. A real gemstone is, by its nature, multifaceted. Perfectly imperfect. It becomes even stronger and more durable under heat and pressure.

That's because GEMs learn to replace perfection with practicality. They are honest enough to admit their limitations, but won't ever give up trying their best. And their best will have to do. Your children won't know any better.

My mother always used to say, "Do your best, and if your best isn't good enough, then so be it." If you do your best and you have nothing else to give, then you still end up crowned with the laurel leaves of life. Let's always aim to give our children a daily dose of this kind of consistent, unconditional love, as well as giving them understanding, validation, and forgiveness (even if one decides to redecorate a bedroom by nailing *library book* covers to the wall).

Just before Casey was born, when I was practically aquiver with anxiety, a very wise woman told me something that immediately put my mind at ease. In fact, I got so much comfort from her words that I've repeated them to every pregnant woman I've ever talked to.

"No one can be a better mother to that child than you can," she told me.

She was right. No one is a better mom to Casey and Cole than yours truly. Sometimes I am wildly successful as a mom. Other times I fail miserably. But each time, they know I am giving it my all. And I also try at least once in a while to treat myself in the same way I treat Casey and Cole—even when I mess up big-time.

A few years back we were trying to survive another fun-filled holiday at Walt Disney World when Casey dragged me over to a kiosk filled with nameplates. "I found yours!" she shouted excitedly. *Wow*, I thought, *that's a surprise*, as René isn't exactly the most common name.

Beaming, Casey handed me the nameplate. It read MOM.

For my kids, I *am* a good-enough mother. I'm doing the best I can. They know it; I know it.

And that's good enough for me!

I

casey and cole:
the rose and the thorn

TO HELP YOU UNDERSTAND ME AND MY PARENTING style (and I *do* think of it as a "style"), allow me to reintroduce the people who've helped me hone it. Though I crave peace and the occasional week-long vacation alone so that I can escape the role of referee for the fights over who ate the last Pop-Tart, I simply cannot imagine my life without my husband, Buff, and my children, Casey and Cole.

I look back on my life pre-children, and I realize that nothing I thought I understood intellectually about raising kids compares with the reality of just doing it. The sheer gravity and magnitude of the responsibility, the fears, the joys—which never go away—can leave you breathless with anxiety, consumed by what-ifs and worst-case scenarios. If you let them.

How is it that Casey and Cole, the pilot and copilot of the bus driving me straight to the funny farm, can also make my heart strain at the seams when I catch a glimpse of them from across the room? Can I keep up with them? They're each so much their own person, a melding of genes from my husband and me, coupled with their unique personalities, likes, and dislikes. Sometimes I look at them and marvel at who they are, where they came from, and what's shaping them as they learn and grow. Casey, my sweet rosebud. Cole, my sweet thorn, who should have been named Get Down From There.

And then, sometimes, I want to wring both of their necks. Like the time they spray-painted a long white streak down the middle of the brown garage.

But that's how life is, isn't it? The very thing that scares the hell out of you is the same thing you want to do, again and again and again. Like jumping out of a moving plane at thirty-three thousand feet, or running to the drugstore for a pregnancy test, hoping against hope the stick will turn pink.

During my first pregnancy my obstetrician said Casey's due date was August 28. The problem was, no one informed *her*, and as the day came and went, my cervix stayed closed tighter than a Ziploc freezer bag. When in the beginning I got a glimpse of Casey, on the first of many ultrasounds I had during her time in utero, I was fascinated. Completely, totally, hopelessly in love with someone who, save the occasional jab in the ribs, I hadn't yet met.

Still, Casey wasn't exactly an ideal tenant, because her idea of fun was partying all night and kicking all day, and I gotta tell you, after forty-two weeks, I weighed more than my husband and I'd had enough. Yes, she was late, and I was cranky. Fast-forward a few days to when I thought I was in labor and the doctor breezily informed me I was not, but said that I should expect all systems to be go within twenty-four hours or so. Buff's response was to go play golf, and mine was to promptly lock myself out of the house. Off I waddled to the neighbor's house to put my feet up and sip on my first glass of chardonnay in nine-and-a-half months. I knew it probably wasn't going to make a dent in Casey's development at forty-two weeks, but it was certainly going to improve my disposition.

Naturally, even though I already felt like a water buffalo, after drinking the chardonnay was when I started to feel truly peculiar. But I couldn't get into the house and I couldn't find Buff, who was busy merrily whacking a few balls. After only a mild bout of freaking-out, I finally reached him, and he came home only to ask me (while I was panting away and nearly ready to keel over because I was so out of breath with the one breathing technique I could remember) if I was *really* in labor, because, after all, the doctor had said I wasn't.

I still made him drive me to the hospital, where I spent the next twenty-seven nonproductive hours in labor. Remarkably, after the resulting C-section from a doctor I'd never seen before but whom I was willing to kiss on the lips after he finally got that kid out of me, my heart, ever-so-Grinch-like, instantly expanded by three sizes the minute I laid eyes on Casey, my sweet-as-spun-sugar angel from on high.

I vividly remember when Casey and I were first introduced. After the nurses cleaned her up and handed my delicious baby burrito (which is what I've always thought swaddled babies look like) to me, I marveled that I had played any role whatsoever in her making. And then a shudder gripped me from the tip of my sweaty, matted hair to my thankfully pristine pedicure.

I thought: *NOW WHAT?*

Because here's the thing: Unlike for your car or microwave or computer, there is no owner's manual provided! Those munchkins come out hollering with it all hanging out—and the nurses hand them to you and leave you to your own devices. Of all the nerve!

I expect you were a lot like me and read all of the books that tell you what to expect during pregnancy and what newborns will be like. But for me Casey's birth was much like exam week at college, when I crammed all night, consuming nothing but black coffee and NoDoz, gripped by the irrational fear that, as soon as I took my seat in the classroom, clutching my number-two pencil, all those answers would instantly fall right through the trapdoor of my cerebral cortex when I needed them most.

So there I lay with my baby burrito in my arms looking up at me as if she were as terrified of this new arrangement as I was.

Naturally, I panicked.

But Casey was such a delightful baby, with such a lovely, easygoing, nondemanding, sunshiny disposition, that Buff and I quickly fell into a regular schedule, and, minus a few toddler moments, it was all fairly smooth sailing. Basking in our success—thinking, ridiculously enough in retrospect, that her nature had something to do with our nascent but clearly already formidable parenting ability—Buff and I decided that we weren't going to have this baby dictate to us. Oh, no. We were already a family unit, and she had joined our family, and nothing was gonna change. We were going to do whatever we wanted, when we wanted to, and Casey was just gonna tag along and be happy about it.

So we took Casey with us everywhere—on trips, to restaurants, shopping, to parties, out with friends. She almost never cried and was good as gold.

Casey was as a baby all those years ago as she is as a

tween now: quiet, sensitive, quick to smile, fairly easygoing, with a wonderful disposition. (Of course, by the time she hits adolescence, I'll be waiting, cringing with despair, for the first time my wonderful daughter will look me full in the eyes and say, "I hate your guts!")

In fact, I should blame her for tricking Buff and me into having another child. She was such a good baby, we thought (mistakenly so), *Oh, what the heck, we are just amazingly great parents. Why not go to the well one more time? Why, this is a snap! In fact, we're almost perfect as parents. Who needs all that gobbledygook you find in baby books? Not us! Why, we should write our own!*

Just as we were busy patting ourselves on the back, the stick turned pink, and life was never ever the same again.

You know, I've faced and conquered many challenges in my life. But that was BC—as in, Before Cole.

Cole Arthur Parham. Little did I know that even though he freeloaded in my womb for thirty-eight weeks, the real work would begin just about the minute he got out. When that boy was snatched from the comfy confines of the womb—he, like his sister, the prior tenant, deigned to move out of his rent-controlled district only because the digs got too small for him—he was a take-no-prisoners kind of baby. In fact, his mantra was "I'm gonna get my way, so don't get in my way."

One of the few problems I'd had with Casey was that she had had trouble suckling, and I'd had to work with a lactation consultant, who had hovered over my breast, cooing and squeezing, trying to entice Casey to latch on.

Cole, on the other hand, never wanted to latch *off*.

The lactation consultant and all those baby books I'd

devoured told me that I should brace myself for the every-two-hours onslaught, as breast milk flies right through babies. So here I was, a scant hour and thirty minutes after feeding Cole, nipples sore, bags bulging under my eyes from no sleep, my hair closely resembling a rat's nest, a toddler clutching one leg, with a kid whose mouth was wide open at every turn and who was gearing up for more. At an hour and forty-five minutes, that boy was ready for food! His stomach would start growling and he would begin to cry. It took only a minute of crying before the battalion was fully engaged and the full-on screaming started. There was no consoling him. So I threw the baby books out the window and shoved the teat into his mouth because I couldn't take it anymore.

Three months later, when I had to go back to work, I cold-turkeyed the daytime milk-fest because I had to be able to fit into my suits (fervently praying every day that the binding I'd wound around myself like a mummy would prevent me from leaking on the five o'clock news). But I still kept up the night-time feeding for a long time, as I'd done with Casey, because it was such a wonderful way to connect with my babies at the end of the day. I always felt like the minute you stopped nursing, any old fool could take care of your baby.

Speaking of fools, that was me, wondering just what the heck was going on with Cole. Not to say that the boy was *difficult* (ha!)—he was just so markedly *different* from Casey. Even when she was only a few months old, we could pretty much keep up our regular routines as a family, because she was such a well-behaved dream in public. As she got older, whenever we went out to eat, she'd sit calmly and quietly in her high chair, coloring and waiting patiently for her food.

Once the food arrived, it would miraculously move from the plate to her mouth without any stops at the floor or my lap. Cole, on the other hand, would squirm in his seat the entire time, spilling salt and sugar everywhere before grabbing a fork or a knife and merrily playing games you rushed to stop before anyone got hurt.

Nearly nine years later not much has changed. I was talking to one of the counselors at Cole's camp last summer—not even one of his own counselors, mind you—and once she realized who I was, all she could say was, "Yeah, that Cole is a wild man."

Take teeth, for example. Casey, being the responsible child, has lost all her teeth in the house, and has come to me for comfort and in happy anticipation of a visit from the tooth fairy and the five bucks she'll discover under her pillow in the morning.

Cole has lost maybe one tooth in the house. The others have literally been lost. Somewhere. Anywhere. Just lost.

Last time that happened, he wrote a note to the tooth fairy:

```
Dear Tooth Fairy,
I lost my tooth AGAIN, and when I find it,
it's going to be your lucky day.
```

Cole is the child my mother warned me about when she was trying to put the fear of God into me. He's the child you'll urge your daughters to steer clear of. Once, when he was about four, he was busy putting on a "show" for us when Casey ran in and announced that she wanted to be in it too.

"Casey," he breezily informed her, "there's only room for one star in this show!"

Actually, Cole is an adorable boy with a bright smile,

dreamy dimples, and huge brown eyes. Buff and I used to joke with each other that he looked like a Volkswagen when he was born, because his eyes literally took up a third of his face! He will, no doubt, charm his way into public office sooner than we all think. He's energetic, headstrong, single-minded—all quantities you want in a world leader.

But not a third grader.

In fact, just the other night he informed me that he wanted to be president.

So I said, "You do?"

"Yep." Then he frowned. "Does the president have to make speeches?"

"Why, yes, he does," I replied.

He shrugged. "Well, I don't really have anything to say."

That's the first and only time he'll ever say *that*! I know I can't control what he's thinking about or what's going to come out of his mouth, any more than I can control Casey's tendency to shy away from the spotlight.

The fact that my children are such polar opposites has taught me a priceless lesson in managing my expectations and minimizing comparisons. Casey's and Cole's personalities are now as they were the minute they emerged from the womb. Casey is quiet, shy, and demure. Cole entered screaming.

And I wouldn't have it any other way.

in the buff

I'VE BEEN MARRIED TO BUFF PARHAM FOR THIRTEEN years, which in and of itself is a miracle.

We were married in January of 1994 for several reasons.

One: He can balance a checkbook.

Two: Unlike me, he is not completely ruled by emotion. Let me tell you—after thirty-one years of *that*, I was exhausted. If I had married one of the other guys I'd dated—the guys who were full of excitement and passionate kisses and empty promises—oh, God, I'd be living in a shelter downtown. I mean, *someone's* got to be the grown-up at least some of the time in any successful relationship. *Someone's* got to remember to pay the bills.

But the biggest reason we married was, of course, love.

I met Buff in 1992, when he was forty-three and I was twenty-nine. (Actually, his real name is James, but when I heard that he'd been nicknamed Buff because he'd run like a buffalo on his college football team, the name stuck!) I was working as a local morning and noontime anchor at the ABC affiliate in Dallas, and he was the station manager there, separated from his wife and with a daughter only ten years younger than I was. He divorced later that year, and several months after that we began dating. After about eight months, we decided, well, you want to get married? Okay, let's get married.

Off we flew to the Bahamas to do the deed. When my mom found out what we were up to, she promptly asked what flight she could get on. I told her, one that was going anywhere but to the Bahamas. Who takes her mother on her honeymoon?

Instead, we paid a couple of witnesses ten dollars each, and the reverend a hundred. I bought my label-free wedding gown at a consignment store for another whopping hundred bucks. The entire union cost less than five hundred dollars.

And that's exactly the way we wanted it!

The beginning of our relationship pretty much forecasted the way the relationship has evolved over the years. Neither of us expected, or indeed wanted, a lovey-dovey, dewy-eyed, drenched-in-grand-passion relationship. We've always been much more interested in growing a marriage that is deeply rooted in love and friendship, yes, but also deeply rooted in practicality.

Which goes to the core of good-enough mothering: If it ain't *practical*, it ain't happening.

Despite our differences in age, experience, and temperament, we coexist on the same page when the fundamental big issues are concerned. We came from similar backgrounds— middle-class, two-parent households where both parents worked long hours and impressed upon us the value of good, honest work. We share the same belief system. In the area of Texas where we lived early in our marriage, some houses are built on what's called a pier-and-beam foundation; instead of pouring down a concrete foundation, the piers are built down into the ground, and then the beams are placed on top. That way there's a little give to the house when the ground starts to shift. It's a clever way to make sure the house doesn't crack apart when the ground moves.

I look at our marriage as having very similar piers and beams, giving us a solid foundation that won't crack apart (by us staying angry, demanding a separation, getting divorced) when the ground moves (we're screaming at each other).

We've always made a conscious effort to have adult conversations. By that I mean something more complicated than where we want Casey and Cole to go to college or how my mother is doing—for instance, meaty conversations about what's happening in the Middle East and what it's going to take to solve that, or why Pluto got demoted from planet status, or what we can do to combat racism.

Whenever we find the time to really talk, I realize that's another part of why I love Buff. He has an unbelievable brain. He's out there, engaged in the world, and he *thinks*. He's someone I can bounce ideas off of. It's really nice to live with someone and have regular talk-fests about issues that do not revolve solely around the kids.

This kind of environment is valuable because both of us want to share with our children how important it is to be contributing members of society, and we want to impress upon them that the world is a very large place and that they'll need to find their positions in it. But having adult talk-fests with Buff is also valuable because a good-enough mother makes sure that life does *not* revolve solely around her kids every waking second. She wants to remain a well-rounded individual, engaged by many important issues outside of parenting that have interested and will continue to interest her.

In addition, Buff and I have a common goal. I remember years ago, when we got engaged, we decided that we wanted our house to be a fortress from the world, an idea we'd impress on any children we might have. That when we went out there and slayed all of the dragons that we had to slay that day, we'd take comfort in the knowledge that as soon as we got home to lick our wounds, we'd be able to pull up the drawbridge and be protected from the howling wolves outside. We're very picky about who we let in—I don't mean into our home, into our *lives*.

Casey and Cole understand this and positively thrive in this atmosphere of safety. They know that if they've had a hard day at school, a hug and a sugar-laden snack will be waiting for them as soon as they race into the house, drop their backpacks, and shout, "Mom! Where are you?"

That doesn't mean that we haven't had our fair share of trouble. Let's just say that the things I was initially attracted to in Buff are precisely those that drive me freaking nuts sometimes. One night I thought my head would pop right off if I heard my name called one more time. Buff, God bless him, is the love of my life, but he simply cannot handle it when anything in his orbit is out of place. (The Virgo in him won't allow it, is his excuse, even though he hasn't read his horoscope in twenty-seven years.) So, naturally, he expected his shaving kit to remain where it's been since the Reagan administration. Forget that we've moved three times in the past decade, or that for some reason we need to clean the bathroom every now and again. Buff couldn't find his shaving kit.

Save the date! The world is ending NOW!

So he was sighing and storming around the house, in a none-too-subtle effort to get me to say soothingly, "Honey, what are you looking for?"

Of course it goes without saying that trying to not sweat it isn't going to work all the time. I once interviewed a relationship expert on *The Early Show* who told me that, basically, having children will rip a marriage apart at the seams. Yeah, that's what I call a positive spin on partnered parenting!

But then I thought about what he'd said, and I realized that, dang it all, he was right. *If you let it.*

Which is why I often ask myself, *Why is it that when you become a good-enough mother, you become a good-enough lover, too?* Seriously, given my hours (I get in the bed by nine p.m. and get up in the middle of the night so I can be out the door at four a.m.) and Buff's erratic schedule, coupled with the fact that our house isn't vast and sprawling, let's just say that Casa Parham is not exactly conducive to a steaming, smoking, hopping sex life.

Look, don't get the wrong idea here. I really love Buff, and I know he loves me and lives with me and puts up with me, and that in itself makes me crazy about him, each and every day.

But, as it was with our marriage ceremony, our deep and abiding feelings for each other have always been a very pragmatic kind of love. Still, it sure was a less pragmatic kind of love back in those now-hazy days of freedom when we were first married.

Remember those glorious days, before poopy diapers, when you had a free Saturday afternoon to do whatever you wanted with your husband? Buff and I would laze around in bed all morning, and then he'd ask me what I wanted to do, and I'd say, "Shoot, I don't know, what do you want to do?"

And he'd say, "Oh, I don't know, do you feel like doing anything?" Only if we were really motivated did we bother to even roll out of bed.

When Casey was born, she was such a divine baby, with a regular schedule and deep sleeping habits, that Buff and I marveled at how little our love life suffered. Sure, I was a lot more tired, but I was also ecstatic that I was a mom, and that Buff and I had created this marvelous little creature together.

But that was BC. Anyone who wanted to avoid the chance of getting pregnant anytime soon could have borrowed little baby Cole for a few weeks, as Buff and I inadvertently discovered. We'd finally find a minute to ourselves, and before the lights went out the screaming would start. I'd then go through the frantic mommy checklist:

> Was Cole tired? No, he should have been asleep
>   an hour ago.
> Was he hungry? No, I had just fed the greedy little squirt.
> Was he wet? No, I had just changed him.
> Was he the world's first exception to the "no baby is
>   intentionally demanding" thing? You bet he was.

I felt about Cole then as I feel about Buff now. Yes, my love for Buff is profound and everlasting. I'm always going to love him. But there are going to be days when I like him, and there are going to be days when the "intentionally demanding" means I like him a whole lot less.

But that's what a relationship is, isn't it—like an accordion.

Sometimes we're very, very close, and sometimes we're far apart. I think that we're at a point now in our relationship where we're really okay with that. I'm okay with Buff and his *whatever*—his quirkiness and his rules and his temper. He's okay with *my* losing it, and my saying that I need space and me-time, as he knows it's not a reflection on him or on our kids. No way am I planning to walk out the door and bolt for good. Being a good-enough mother means I can bolt down the driveway to go for a run when Buff and the kids have rung my bell so many times it looks like that cracked old thing in Philadelphia.

Okay, confession time. I have my own issues, including a temper with a capital *T*. Don't cross me, because it's hard for me to forgive; and when I do forgive, it's almost impossible to forget. Which means that sometimes Buff and I just blow, winding up with shouting matches loud enough to scatter the squirrels, because our lives are so hectic that we snap from the stress.

We do try to save those for behind closed doors, but the kids are smart. That coupled with their ears next to the door, and they'll sometimes overhear what we're trying to keep private. "Don't fight, don't fight!" they'll shriek. Of course, we might not even be fighting, but are having what I like to call "spirited discussions." Kids can't often tell the difference, though, so when we know that the kids have overheard a spat and are upset, we make sure they see us resolve our conflicts calmly. This isn't important just for Buff and me but for the kids, too, as they're going to have to become comfortable with their own emotions, needs, and tempers as they grow older.

I think it's also crucial to reassure the kids that we're a

team, the Parham team, and team members don't quit on one another, no matter what. Even when one teammate messes up, you don't kick him or her off the team because he or she messed up. You hunker down in a huddle and you work together. You apologize, figure out what you have to do for your team, and try again.

And we honestly try to abide by the "never go to bed angry" rule.

See, I *always* try to save my sweat for the big stuff. Like notes from Cole's teacher, which are guaranteed to leave me a gibbering, blubbering mass of exposed synapses.

But the rest is piddly stuff, because at the end of the day, I do know that Buff's proud of me. Plus I know that he, more than anyone else, believes in me and what I can get done. Especially when he watches me on television; he thinks that I practically created the concept of talking heads! What truly matters is that whenever we need to, we can sit down with each other and just talk. Like grown-ups. About everything and nothing.

We made a decision early on to take the time, every once in a while, to go back and talk about our dreams and goals and aspirations. Time goes by in a blink, and the kids grow and change and become more cognizant of the world, and we need to grow with them. We're partners.

But no partnership sustains itself in a vacuum. It's hard work. Sure, we make plans and have goals, but we're still adult enough to recognize that life is a fluid thing—it moves and shifts and evolves—and you need to make sure you don't get stuck. If you keep your spirit open (and your temper in check), you'll be free to say "I Don't Care" and realize that you mean it!

And when Buff knows I need to hear it, or even when I don't, he'll be the first one to tell me, "You know what? This is so great for you. I'm really proud. You did a terrific job."

Buff is also big enough to understand my needs and give me space. His generosity gives me the sense that, no matter where I go or what I have to do for work or for myself or for our kids, I'll always have a safe haven waiting for me when I need it the most. I couldn't ask for anything more rock-solid and loving than that.

Plus, absence makes the heart grow fonder. The fact that Buff's away as much as he is on work-related business helps minimize any quarreling. Not that we don't argue. Oh, brother, do we ever. We're just not around each other enough to keep the fights going!

Unless Buff arrives home in the middle of the night, road-weary and longing for the minute when he can collapse. Up the stairs he trudges, wanting nothing more than to lie down comfortably in his own bed, next to his wife . . . when he discovers his place has been usurped by two small pillow-hogging maniacs.

Okay, I confess: Both kids crawl into bed with me when Buff's away. They just want to cuddle and be near me, and I'm okay with that, except that when I say "be near me," I mean that they want to be *on top* of me.

Still, I appreciate the fact that Casey will sprawl over the foot of the bed and Cole will sleep with his head on my shoulder, because I know that all too soon the thrill will be gone, and when that happens, I'll shed many tears knowing that my kids have grown up for good.

Buff, not surprisingly, is counting the days.

Since our time together is so precious, Buff and I try to have date nights, but they're too few and far between. Usually our date nights include the kids. Which is not exactly a date night. As soon as Casey and Cole have finished cramming the food into their faces, in between interrupting us, they're like, "Okay, we're ready to go."

"Excuse me? We're still eating here," I'll say.

Blessed silence for thirty seconds.

"Mom, are you done yet?" one of them will ask.

So Buff and I try to steal away several times a year, just for a weekend or so, to not have *restaurantus interruptus* and to have a little we-time. Then we instantly remember how much fun we have when we're together. We have a really strong friendship, and intimacy within that friendship, so that no matter how much we drive each other crazy, we manage to muddle through.

And maybe, just maybe, we won't always need to haul out the BlackBerries on one of those romantic getaways. You know, to make an appointment for sex three weeks hence, assuming, naturally, that we'll be able to book a babysitter in time.

Yep, *Think of the we-time and romantic getaways*, was what I tried to remind myself when I glanced down at the computer one day when I was on the air. Buff had just e-mailed me about the babysitter. Because I'm out the door at four a.m. and because Buff needs to leave for work at seven thirty, our trusted babysitter, Consuelo, arrives by seven a.m. to get the kids off to school or camp on those days when Buff can't take them.

Consuelo is late, said his message.

Have I mentioned that I was on the air? That, um, I was on the air at the *same time* every Monday through Friday?

I was, like, *Hello out there, turn on your TV. You see that woman who looks a lot like your wife? Dang, it is your wife! And I'm broadcasting live to three-million-plus viewers, so I'm really sorry but I just cannot handle the babysitter crisis right now. You deal with it!*

Or let's just say that sometimes Buff's imagination fails him. He called me the other day as I was having a moment to myself after a long, much-needed workout, sauntering over to my favorite store (Target) to pick up (fat-laden) snacks Casey and Cole needed for camp.

"CAN YOU PLEASE ADD BAND-AIDS TO YOUR LIST?" he shouted, clearly agitated. "I REALLY NEED THEM!"

"Omigod, what's the matter?" I quickly asked, my heart racing.

"Well, I cut my finger pretty bad," he told me.

"Should I go to a drugstore? Or do you need stitches?"

"No, Target's fine," he replied. "I just need a Band-Aid that doesn't have Xena the Warrior Princess on it."

3

i don't care

BACK IN THOSE BEST-FORGOTTEN FORMATIVE years, I was a huge old wallflower, as tall as I am now (5'7") but about forty pounds lighter, give or take an ounce. Add to the mix ugly glasses, crooked teeth, stilts for legs, and zits, and I quickly realized that I needed to rely on something other than my appearance to help me make friends.

Which is why I developed a wicked sense of humor. I had to; it was a purely instinctive survival mechanism. I was such a funny-looking beanpole that I figured I might as well *be* funny too.

Honing a sense of humor is critical to getting through life's daily muddles and puddles, and it is also critical to the essence of the good-enough mother philosophy. Life is hard—and I know it's even harder when you have kids. A sense of humor when everything is falling down around you helps make the crash less painful. And it can often make just about everything and everyone bearable.

I know that some of you might feel that what I'm about to say is blasphemous, but the thing is, cutting myself a little slack does *not* mean that I'm giving my kids less. In fact, I think I'm giving them *more*—because I'm showing them how to balance and handle whatever the situation du jour is, and how to react appropriately when all hell breaks loose. I mean, what else can you do when your kid walks in with a whistle stuck up his nose so he can blow a tune?

If I had a kid like Cole and I *didn't* have a sense of humor, trust me, I'd do everything in my power to develop one, pronto!

I know I'm happy and I have a ready smile even though my life is pretty crazy. For me, laughing through life is like emotional Botox. The more you laugh, the less likely you are to frown and become an old crabby Appleton. Laughter needs to be an essential ingredient in everyone's daily diet.

There's a time for play and a time for work, a time to be serious and a time to lighten up. When I'm on TV and dealing with serious, life-threatening news and issues affecting the world we live in, I can deal with it. And when I'm on vacation with the kids, I can happily join them as they clamber up the enormous slides in the water park, and scream my head off all the way down.

Okay, so I'm an overgrown kid at heart—but my gung-ho attitude means I was usually the one given the goofy, physical, on-air segments to do at work. I'd hate to not get to race a soap box derby car (never mind how hard it was to squeeze my butt into that thing, or that I nearly crashed into our hundred-thousand-dollar cameras). Or swim in frigid water with beluga whales. I'm really happy that I do have a healthy sense of "Okay, I'll give it a try." I'll give anything a try *once*.

I hope I never have to tell my kids I'm too old to do something crazy with them. They want to go blading, I'm there.

They want to climb up the scaling wall, I'm strapping on the harness. Even though I clearly remember how mortified I'd get when my own mom used to do what I perceived at the time as crazy things. Mom would talk to anyone on the street. Strangers, anybody, it didn't matter—she'd just strike up a conversation, and I'd cringe with embarrassment. And now I find myself doing that, with my own mortified kids hollering at me to cut it out, and I think, *Oh my God, I'm turning into my mother!*

So, given my druthers, I'd rather laugh about it.

Just the other day, for example, I called the kids down for dinner, and Cole showed up in the dining room, stark naked save for several of my silk scarves strategically draped over his private parts.

"Cole, what the hell are you doing?" I asked, laughing.

"I'm an Indian and this is how they dress," he told me with a shrug.

"I see," I replied.

So, did I send him upstairs to put his clothes back on? Did I chastise him for scattering what I knew had been a drawer-ful of carefully folded (for once) and clean (for once) silk scarves that he knew he wasn't supposed to scatter?

Nope. I handed him a napkin.

And when he complained that his rear end was getting cold, I merely rearranged one of the scarves to cover his butt cheeks. "Now eat," I said, laughing even more. "Your dinner is getting cold."

Now, I suppose that some people think I'm too permissive or too immature or too silly, and I have to admit that sometimes my husband is one of those people. Take the time the kids built a makeshift fortress out of sheets, blankets, and towels in Cole's bedroom. Buff took one look and said, "What happened to the sheets? The towels are all over the place. Where did this mess come from?" Whereas I looked at it and thought it was a phenomenal example of how well they had used their imaginations.

Believe me, there was some serious talking going on that night once the kids went to bed. I told Buff that criticizing our kids' passion for imaginative play was not going to happen again, and that one thing I would truly love is for him to try to remember what it was like to be eight or nine. Not the nine-year-old boy he was forced to become in order to help take care of his family—but the nine-year-old he could have been if his life had been a little bit more carefree and his innate personality not quite so rigid. I wanted him to reconnect with his inner child. Not just because I think it would make him happier, but because the inner child in me—the one always lurking right below the surface—wants a playmate!

A playmate who loves to laugh as much as I do.

So, getting back to those boring old souls who think I'm too much of a goof-bucket. Or maybe they can't relate to my sense of humor, or understand my good-enough mother message.

For them, I have a very simple mantra: I Don't Care.

I worried for years about what people thought of me, not just colleagues or friends but also the Dreaded Super-Moms at school, or snarky moms in the line at the super-market, who were frowning at Cole's begging for Hot Wheels, baseball cards, and a PlayStation all at the same time. You know what? Worrying about what other people think is a total waste of time.

Repeat the GEM mantra after me: I Don't Care.

Let me tell ya, freeing yourself from worrying about the things over which you have no control—let's say, perhaps, your child sneaking a forbidden piece of bubble gum into her mouth after brushing her teeth, kissing you good night, and turning off the lights, so it ends up all over her hair in the morning—is extremely liberating.

It gives you lots more time to think of creative ways to explain to others why two inches of your child's hair are missing and why the kids need to go to the dentist more than twice this year.

Of course, there are important things I do worry about in my own little orbit. I have always worried about what my bosses have thought of my performance at work. I want viewers to know and believe that I'm smart and informed and capable of doing a good job. And as my husband always says, I care about five people: the people under this roof, and Tracy, his daughter from his first marriage. In truth, I care about the people under other roofs too—my mom (the kids' only surviving grandparent), my sister, Tracy, and her family, and my friends and colleagues. And it goes without saying that we're concerned about how we behave and that our kids grow up with rock-solid values to be contributing members of society.

All that other stuff is just bunk!

Repeat the GEM mantra one more time: I Don't Care.

Which is how I can shrug off the small stuff and laugh.

Even when Cole spits on his pizza and informs me that he's marking his territory!

4

that'll get you ten to twenty: crimes and punishments

TO SAY THAT BUFF AND I VIEW PARENTING IN the same way is like saying you'd see the same sights on tour bus rides through heaven and hell.

I'm the balloon and he's the string.

Buff is what the young kids would call old school. It's his way or the highway.

Whereas I'm more touchy-feely, he's more the strict disciplinarian.

Whereas I'm more spontaneous, he's more methodical.

Whereas I'm the soft touch, and don't see the harm in occasionally allowing Casey and Cole to eat a few gummy worms before dinner as long as they clear their plates, he tells the kids, "No way." The rules are the rules and no explanation will be forthcoming.

When the kids question why—because that's what kids do—I launch into a *War and Peace*–like explanation, figuring that once Casey's and Cole's eyes glaze over, I'll get my way. Buff, on the other hand, will respond with that old chestnut, "BECAUSE I SAID SO," without a second thought. Fortunately, I know that Buff and I are on the same page when the big issues are concerned. We're different sides of the same coin; the hoped-for outcome (Cole and Casey actually listening to us and doing what they're told) is the same. As a result, we approach discipline techniques from our own perspectives. And in order to understand our discipline styles, first you've got to understand a little bit more about my husband.

Buff was raised in a house full of love in Pasadena, but times were tough. His mom was a nurse and his dad was a truck driver, and the two had work hours of the "ships that pass in the night" variety. His dad would cook breakfast and put it on the counter before he had to leave for work at five in the morning, and his mom wouldn't be home from her shift until seven. There was a two-hour period every morning when little nine-year-old Buff was in charge of getting his younger sister out of bed, fed, and ready for school. He had to grow up too fast. Couple this with Buff's innate personality, which teeters on the side of strict responsibility and by-the-book rules. Then throw in my innate playful, carefree personality, and you've got me bringing Buff a zest for life, while he brings me the stern dad who tells me it's time to grow up and pay those bills.

Let's just say that we're a couple with a few boundaries to establish when it comes to disciplining our kids!

It is a bit of a problem when Buff says "BECAUSE I SAID SO" and doesn't acknowledge that his not explaining why to the kids will likely have consequences, but I have to admit I sometimes secretly delight whenever Casey and Cole refer to their beloved daddy as the Mean Man.

Yep, he's the Mean Man.

Consuelo is fond of telling me that if the kids are doing

something naughty and she says, "I'm going to call your mom," they'll hand her the phone. But if she says, "I'm going to call your dad," they stop right away. So there is something to the Mean Man syndrome. It works like a charm when I need them to clean up some fresh mess. All I have to say is something along the lines of, "You know Daddy is going to flip out if he comes home and sees that."

On the other hand I'm never too thrilled when someone gets into trouble in the house after I've already reprimanded him or her. Enter the Mean Man, who can't prevent himself from coming in to reprimand Casey or Cole all over again, sometimes going on for what seems like an hour. I'm like, *Okay, it's over. We got it.*

Buff has impressed upon me the usefulness of "Don't talk past the close." That's salesman-ese for "Once all the parties have agreed upon a set price, shut your piehole!"

But Buff hasn't yet perfected the GEM mantra of "I Don't Care," and he sometimes has trouble dropping the bone he's been gnawing. One Saturday night we were all going to the movies, and there was practically a monsoon outside. Buff told Cole to get his jacket because it was wet and chilly, so Cole asked if he could wear my jacket. Not a nice jacket but my ratty, puffy blue workout jacket that was so big on him it fell practically to his calves. To me, it was no big deal, so I said yes without a second's thought. Out we ran through the pelting raindrops to the car, got in, and shook ourselves dry, then looked around for Buff. A few minutes passed. No Buff. Out I ran back to the house, wondering what the heck was going on.

And where was Buff? Up in Cole's room looking for one of Cole's jackets.

"Buff, what are you doing?" I asked him. "We're going to be late for the movie."

"Cole needs to wear his own jacket," he said in a huff.

"Oh, for God's sake, what does it matter? Who cares if Cole wears it?"

"I care, that's who!"

I think what bothered Buff the most wasn't so much the jacket being too big, but that giving in to Cole wearing it went against the rules. Or rather, *Buff's* rules. I'm pretty lax when it comes to the rules in my house. Not the rules about things that are important, like homework, or manners, or no hitting, or anything that could potentially harm anyone.

When it comes to the rest, you guessed it: I Don't Care.

Naturally, what the kids do is play both sides against the middle. So I have to pick my battles, and when I think Buff is being unduly harsh I call him on it. When that happens, my mantra is: What Would Be the Harm in That?

What I believe is most crucial is for our kids to grow up knowing there's a safety net of our love and support and encouragement, not a safety harness. A harness keeps you stuck in one place. A net lets you soar. It'll catch you when you fall.

I'm sure that all of you have seen plenty of examples of what educators refer to as "helicopter parents." You know, the kind that are always hovering because they can't bear the thought of their little princes and princesses failing. They can't let go of the harness.

Yet, failure is one of the most potent teachers. I fail my own standards when I scream and shout. My kids fail when they act out. But it's my job to be good enough to teach them how to make their own choices—and sometimes these *will* be the wrong choices—and how to learn from their mistakes.

I've always been a fan of macro-consequences. I had a teacher who told me that his daughter wanted to stay up late one night, and he said, "Fine, you can stay up as late as you want, but you're still going to have to get up and go to school on time." She stayed up until five in the morning, and could barely drag herself out of the house in time for school. She felt like complete and utter crap all day, but guess what? She never did that again.

Once when we were all out playing miniature golf, Cole, being Cole, wanted to do it his way. Buff wanted him to play by the rules. So what had started out as a fun family outing quickly degenerated into a battle of wills and a discipline situation. I asked Buff what would be the harm in the grand scheme of things if Cole wielded the club like a bowling ball? Ultimately, Cole would have figured out that his method would have meant losing big-time, and that there was a reason golf has been played a certain way for centuries, because it works only if and when you line the ball up *this* way. (And, as any frustrated golfer will tell you, not always then!)

I wish Buff didn't care so much about the rules. But he does. A lot. So does my mom. This is one of my pet peeves, because my mother can't drop the bone either, driving me absolutely crazy when she comes to visit and turns into Little Miss Echo. We'll be going somewhere, and I'll say, "Casey, get your shoes on," and my mother will go, "Yeah, get your shoes, we're ready to go."

Or I'll say, "Cole, cut it out this instant," and she'll say, "Cole, you cut it out this instant and I mean it!"

Exasperated, I tell her that my kids have only one mom, and it's *me*. *You're the grandma.*

Of course, none of that much matters, because for whatever reason, my kids don't really listen to her, or to me, either. She could scream her head off and it wouldn't make a dent.

My kids—and all kids—needs parents to be parents, not equals. Trust me, I'm not one of these parents who go around gushing that their kids are their best friends. Is your best friend eight years old? I don't think so.

And parents who are *parents*, not best friends, have rules. We run a benevolent dictatorship in our house. There is no democracy, really. Those little people make most of the noise and most of the mess, but since they don't contribute to the big pot that we call a mortgage, their voting privileges are nil.

So when Cole tells me he's going to run away, I offer to help him pack his bags!

Seriously, though, one of the hardest parts of being a parent is being able to listen calmly when basically all you want to do is wring your little darling's neck.

Listening and acknowledging are the best weapons in the discipline arena. Children should be treated as equals in this regard, since showing them that their explanation, however convoluted, has been heard is crucial to their sense of validation. No child, even those who are very small, likes to have his or her feelings dismissed. What they did in the first place might not have been the right thing to do, in which case I will come down on them but good, but I try never to pass judgment until I've taken the time and the consideration to calmly listen to what they have to say.

If you're wrong, an apology is a must. Really, what's the

harm in falling on your sword and admitting you blew it? I know plenty of grown-ups who still have a hard time uttering the *S* word (you know, "sorry"), whether they need to say it to their peers or to their kids. I don't get that. I don't see an apology as a sign of weakness, but rather, one of strength.

So if (oh, okay, *when*) I blow my stack, or if my kids catch me doing something I shouldn't be doing, I like to think that I'm big enough to say that I'm sorry, and that I was wrong. Just the other day, Cole said to me, "Mom, you know when you ask me or Casey to close your door? You *never* say please." I realized he was right and apologized. I remembered to say please that night, and every single time after that.

A good-enough mother knows when to apologize, because she knows that's how her kids are going to learn. Accept what you've done wrong and move on.

Knowing how easy it is for adults to blow it always sets a great example for kids, even in their own peer groups. If they make a mistake, it's a lot easier for them to say, "You were right, I was wrong" without any shame if they've already heard Mom easily saying that herself.

I discuss this with Buff till I'm blue in the face, and when I do, he says, "You're right and I shouldn't have done that," but it's still not instinctive behavior with him. Stopping the "Because I said so" routine is like learning another language. Buff will catch himself the very next time, and apologize. And the time after that? Right back to square one.

Cole, as you know by now, never saw a boundary he didn't want to leap, scale, or shred. He's not the kind of kid you ever tell not to do something, because he'll blithely go right ahead and do it anyway, just to get your goat. Where Casey is a svelte silver hammer, Cole is a wrecking ball.

I have such a hard time with Cole, because Cole is me!

As a result, the thing that's so darn frustrating is that when I'm disciplining Cole, I'm basically disciplining myself. He knows all the tricks; I guess it's in his DNA, because obviously the lion's share of his genetic material is from me. What's been particularly difficult for me, though, is when he acts out in public. No matter how much a good-enough mother knows that a flailing and screaming kid in a full-bore temper tantrum in the produce aisle isn't really about *her*, and that all kids lose it outside at some point or other, it's almost impossible to separate your own ego from the public scorn and embarrassment when you know you're being judged solely by the flailing and screaming.

And automatically being judged a *failure*.

When that happens, I try to repeat my "I Don't Care" mantra until I'm sick of my own voice, and I try not to take the withering stares personally.

As for punishment, once Casey and Cole were old enough to understand, I moved on to the battle-tested time-out. Casey rarely needed them, but Cole sure did.

And yes, a time-out is usually pretty effective. Except that my son, now and then, will sit in the corner and yell, "Is it time to get up yet?"

A minute later: "Is it time to get up yet?"

Again and again until the time-out is up and I'm glad as heck that it is.

What works most effectively, now that they're a little older, is to explain why they aren't going to do whatever it was they wanted to do but knew was naughty. If I take the time to explain it rationally, they might not like it, but they *get* it.

And if that doesn't work, what does work is to take stuff away. I'm a big fan of the stick and carrot approach, although I'm still not sure which is a more powerful incentive, the stick or the carrot! Still, I hate trying to think of punishment on the fly, because it has to be effective for any dents to be made in Cole's thick hide. Hiding all the soda he loves more than life itself (my bad, I know) is not a real punishment. Taking away the PlayStation for a week sure was drastic, and the look on Cole's face would have moved a stone to tears, but he got the message: Actions have consequences and I *will* follow through. I'm not going to just threaten you with doing something that'll hurt. I'm going to *do* it.

Of course, Cole has such a short attention span that he was soon on to the next thing to set my teeth on edge.

I do wonder if any kind of punishment or discipline is effective with Cole, because he has inherited a walloping dose of my "I Don't Care" philosophy. Is what I take such great pains to explain to him merely going in one ear and out the other? Does he get it? Does he care? Sometimes I just don't know with that boy. I'll tell him he needs to be serious—on the odd occasions when he does need to be, like in church—while knowing full well that there's not a serious bone in his body.

When he was four, we were on our annual jaunt to Walt Disney World, this time with Buff's daughter, Tracy, helping out because Buff was stuck on a business trip (his feeble excuse for getting out of having to suffer through "It's a Small World" for the umpteenth time). One day we went to Animal Kingdom, and the blistering heat did us in, so Tracy and I asked the kids what they wanted to do, and they told us that all they wanted was to go to the hotel and swim in the pool. (Which, of course, we could have done in Picketfenceville, but never mind that.) When we got close to the car, it suddenly dawned on me that Cole had an ice cream treat melting in his hand and ice cream streaks all over his face.

"Cole, where did you get that?" I shrieked.

Without missing a lick of his ice cream, he pointed over to the ice cream cart that he'd pinched it from, way back inside the park.

I launched into my *War and Peace*–like explanation of why what he'd done was stealing, and how bad it is to steal, and that he shouldn't ever, ever do it again, but I knew my lesson in morals fell upon deaf ears, since his only concern was eating the ice cream before it melted completely.

I once interviewed a therapist and we discussed childhood memories—what events stay with us as we grow older. He told me that, in his experience, most people seek therapy thanks to their mothers, and for one simple reason—they have the most intimate contact with their mothers during their formative years.

Well, when I heard that, I confessed to him that I was trying hard to be hyperaware of how I speak to my kids so they don't grow up to hate me. He said, "The things that they'll remember from their childhoods will be the things that didn't even register with you."

I nearly choked on my decaf when I heard that, because I didn't agree with him at all. Good-enough mothers know that parenting is *visceral*. You parent the way you were parented, and then you take the things that you did and didn't like and you expand on them. And you still know that your own kids will end up talking about you the way I'm talking about my mother in this book.

Which is precisely what another mom, Chaia, told me. "I was reading to my daughter recently while my husband and son were out getting groceries. You know, one of those warm and cozy mother-daughter moments with her snuggled up to me. She put her arms around my neck and whispered in the most loving of tones, 'Mom, I forgive you for everything that you've done to me.'"

So when it comes to discipline, a good-enough mother will try to find a happy medium. And if she's married to her polar opposite, as I am, she should still be able to say, *Well, he thinks I'm too easy and I think he's too tough, but we must be doing something right because at the end of the day, our kids are still pretty cool.*

Yet, just before you drift off to sleep, or maybe right after some discipline situation, it's really hard, even for someone as laid-back as I am, to not wonder if I handled things in the best possible way. And then my good-enough mother training kicks in, and I remind myself that I did the best I could under the circumstances, and I did what I thought was right, and I'm open to being corrected, and next time I'll try to do better. That's all you can do, really.

And realize that in the morning the "What are you thinking?" will begin again.

As in, Cole opened a pack of mints and began throwing them into the fan to watch them go zinging across the room.

I, showing the appropriate amount of shock and horror, immediately said, "What are you thinking?"

"It's just a plastic fan," Cole told me.

And so for his nice plastic punishment, I took away his plastic PlayStation discs for the day.

pinocchio's pals

IN A MOMENT OF UTTER WEAKNESS, AND because I'm a slave to the madness that is the marketing machine in our advertising-drenched society, I one day (stupidly) bought five twelve-pack cases of soda, thinking (stupidly) that I would dole them out only for special occasions and such. I hauled them out of the car, (stupidly) put them in the pantry in plain view, and laid down strict ground rules to Casey and Cole. As in, only one soda per day.

Right off the bat, there went the whole "special occasion" thing.

"ONE SODA PER DAY!" I told the kids in my sternest voice. I even made them look into my eyes and read my lips. "I shouldn't even let you have that, but I'm treating you, so it's ONE SODA PER DAY!" After all, it was the summer of sugar and TV. "Do you both understand me? Have I made myself perfectly clear?"

Casey nodded vigorously. So did Cole. I (stupidly) believed them and went along on my merry way.

Two days later, Casey came up to me. "Cole's working on his second soda today," she said, thrilled that she could get her brother in trouble.

"COLE! GET DOWN HERE!" I shouted. When he ambled into the kitchen, with nary a sheepish look on his face, I asked if he'd had two sodas. At first he lied. Then he confessed.

"I thought sodas at camp didn't count," he said.

I sighed. "You know what, soda is soda. And it turns out that you had three sodas today—one at camp that you weren't supposed to have, and one extra soda at home. Which means you can't have a soda tomorrow because you had tomorrow's soda today."

"Okay," he said brightly, thinking I was placated and that he was off the hook, when the boom came down.

"And because you not only disobeyed me by having three sodas today but also *lied* to me about it, no PlayStation for three days."

At which point the smarty-pants grin left his face.

Okay, I know that all kids fib at some point or another—and some ages are more notorious than others for the ease with which whoppers come sliding out—and I (stupidly) should have known better than to tempt Mr. Butterfingers with easy proximity to forbidden fruit.

After all, Cole basically started singing the "I didn't do it" chorus as soon as he could talk.

Even Casey, who's usually good as gold, slips up from time to time. Just the other day I came home to find that someone had written with something all over the patio, in really beautiful, flowing cursive lettering, and I asked Casey and Cole who was responsible for that masterpiece. I already knew the answer, because Cole can wield a remote control with more finesse than he can write.

"Did you write on the patio?" I asked Casey, looking her right in the eye.

"Do you like it?" she asked.

"First I need to know, did you do it?"

"I don't remember, but do you like it?"

Here we go, here we go!

"Look, you're not in trouble," I gently told her, "but you will be if you don't tell me the truth. I need to know what you wrote with so I can find out if it'll come off."

At which point the tears began, and they were copious.

So we sat down and had a nice long cuddle, and I told her how crucial it was to be truthful in life. And that being truthful defines who you are. And that we're Parhams. Lying is not something that Parhams do. Lying is absolutely forbidden in our home.

Casey, being the kind of child who is by nature obedient and concerned with doing the right thing, even when she can't help herself from misbehaving once in a blue moon, understands this instinctively. Cole, on the other hand, is so headstrong and so determined to get his own way that he's constantly topping his last whopper with something more creative. I know that a large part of his fibbing stems from the fact that he has such a vivid imagination. He doesn't think, *How can I not get into trouble?* He gaily goes ahead to get into trouble, then asks himself, *How can I get away with it now?*

I suppose I'd be more worried about Cole if I didn't know that underneath the whoppers and the weaseling-his-way-out was a boy with a good heart and a good spirit. I can't tell you how often he's lied about his homework, saying he has done it when he hasn't. When pressed, he gives the stock answer heard by millions of moms around the globe: "I forgot."

Naturally, I don't really believe for a nanosecond that he forgot. The punishment is swift and merciless: He gets grounded, with no TV.

Is that a deterrent? Obviously not, since I get another note from Mrs. Henry, Cole's long-suffering teacher, about the homework. Yet again, I confront him. Yet again, he smiles at me, his big brown eyes brimming with (mock) consternation.

"I forgot," he says.

Yet in the long, tangled thicket of Cole's fibs, he's never said or done anything malicious or lied to cover up having done something that was terribly wrong (like hurting another child or riding his scooter where I said he couldn't because it's dangerous).

I just have to wade through layers of muck to find the Cole I know is there!

And when he does come up with a whopper, it's usually pretty funny, which makes it hard to keep a straight face when he's pulling a fast one. For instance, let's go back to the soda I (stupidly) bought. A few days after the three-soda situation, Cole, whose middle name should have been Shameless, wheedled his way over to me and asked if he could have a soda. I immediately told him no.

"Well, can I have a Lipton Iced Tea, because it's not really a soda?"

Cole would make a great spin doctor. He's already got the knack for rearranging the same words to ask the same question ad infinitum.

Where fibbing can get tricky is when you have to cover up

your own little white lies—you know, the kinds of things you have to say to be polite, especially to avoid hurting other grown-ups' feelings (such as declining invitations to events you know will be more painful and boring than standing in line at the airport to go through security for an international flight). Kids have a built-in radar that can sniff out an anomaly in no time at all. If you have to fib, be sure you've got a story planned so they'll believe you, but be prepared for a lot of (justifiable) anger if they find out you've betrayed their confidence. And if you space a playdate, which we've all done, don't make up an excuse. Just put it out there, say you're sorry that you messed up, that you'll make it up to them, and try to do better next time.

Telling tales is also tricky when it comes to fantasy figures like the tooth fairy and Santa Claus. Although Casey and Cole haven't caught me in a lie yet, I know the clock is ticking toward the sad, sad day when their bubble of trust is going to burst. Hard as it may be to believe, my kids still think Santa is real. They still want so badly to believe. I'm not looking forward to the day—which I fear may be very soon—when my kids leave the final bit of true childhood behind. There's an inevitable shift in perception with maturity. Part of that is realizing that even Mom is fallible. I know kids' realization of this is one of the hardest things about seeing your kids grow up, along with the first sprouting of hair on their legs, and I try to delude myself that I've been warming Casey and Cole (and myself) up to that all along.

But maybe it won't be so bad. Cole will doubtless realize that he can hit me up for even more toys once Santa is out of the picture.

And I can take heart from Good-Enough Mother Chaia, whose daughter, Deana, is about to turn ten. She's changed a lot, but maybe not as much as her mother thought she would. One night at bedtime Deana turned off her lamp and something fell.

"What was that?" Chaia asked.

"Just my imagination," Deana said.

"If it was *your* imagination, why did *I* hear it?" Chaia wanted to know.

"Well, my imagination sometimes gets out of my head," Deana replied without missing a beat. "It comes out through my ears—that's why sometimes I don't hear you so clearly."

high-def is my life

A LARGE PURPLE DINOSAUR SAVED MY LIFE.

Or rather, Barney kept me from stinking up the house.

I mean, when you're a new mom and you've got that cute little bouncy seat and your cute little baby bouncing merrily in it . . .Well, you know that baby-distracting bouncy seat is great and all, but you've still got to get in the shower long enough to shave your armpits and legs, and that ain't gonna happen if you're counting on entertainment from the bouncy seat alone. Result: Hosannas when you play the purple dinosaur from time to time.

I'm not ashamed to admit that had it not been for my favorite large purple dinosaur on the TV, I never would have gotten in the shower, gotten dressed, and gotten out of the house for the first nine months of Casey's life.

I've been working in television for nearly all my adult life—certainly for as long as my kids have been alive—so my being overly critical about TV is rather like biting the hand that feeds me. So far, television has been pretty good to me. You see this nice house, kids? This is the house that TV built!

In fact, there was a time when Casey and Cole thought

everyone's mommy talked to them out of that little box they gazed at with such fascination in the living room.

Seriously, though, as a reporter and as a concerned mom, I've seen the studies and studied the reports on how too much TV can lead to a host of undesirable things, such as childhood obesity and attention deficit disorder. And I believe it. But let's get real for just a moment. Like most other moms, I do worry that my kids consume a little too much of what's coming out of the big plasma box. Kidding aside, I do not believe in TV as a regular babysitter, but we've all done it at one point. If you're like me, you'll have to admit that sometimes you wish your kids would just SIT DOWN and quietly watch something.

For example, the other day I arrived home from work only to see Cole pulling Casey as she straddled Buff's new rolling suitcase, leaving deep gouges across my newly refinished maple floors. The night before that incident, I'd caught them taking turns hauling each other across the floors on my 800-thread-count sheets (naturally, the one and only set of sheets I ever splurged on). It was then that I yanked out a significant chunk of hair from each side of my head as I shouted, "Will you kids PULEEZ sit down and watch some *Xiaolin Showdown*?"

Television, like most things in life, is just fine in moderation.

Precisely how much is too much? Well, isn't that the question for the ages . . . and if you're looking for me to give you the all-time definitive answer, you may as well keep moving, as there's nothing to see here, folks. My guess is as good as yours. Dealing with television is all about balance. And the key, to me, lies in your finding the balance by trusting yourself. You know instinctively how much TV is good enough for your kids—just as you know instinctively how much sugar is good for them, and you know instinctively how much time they can be apart from you.

What works for *me* is that I don't let my kids watch more than an hour a day—and only after all homework is done—during the school year.

But I make Casey and Cole do 1,426 sit-ups while watching, so they don't get sedentary.

I am way more lax during summer months. Isn't that what summer is for? Synonymous with "fun," right? Staying outside until the streetlights come on, lounging on the porch with your friends before jumping up to run around in the yard, making lanyards (and a mess), eating candy until your belly is distended, and sitting in a stupor in front of the TV until your eyes glaze over.

Nowadays my kids, having learned from their father the magic of TiVo and how to manage the universal remote control, can sit zombielike, their complexions glowing in the toxic ultraviolet glow of the tube, for blissfully long summertime hours.

Of course, you know the kids are watching too much when product placement gleaned from the yammering and hectoring in endless commercials becomes a part of their daily dialogue. It was especially disconcerting when Cole and I were in the waiting room at our orthodontist's office, where I contribute monthly to Dr. Schleuter's kids' college fund. While looking at Cole's big teeth, squeezing their way into the space once occupied by chompers a third that size, I said to him, "Hey, buddy, I think you're gonna be a candidate for braces, sooner rather than later. Those teeth are looking a little cramped."

Without looking up, Cole said, "I want Invisalign!"

And that's not all. Casey and Cole have bought hook, line, and sinker into the wonders of Floam, are convinced their lives would be better if they ate Fruit by the Foot (which, as you know, is strategically placed at kids' eye level in your local supermarket), and feel totally deprived if I don't at least offer to check out the Minimoto (which, for the blessedly uninformed, is a motorized pool toy) and, hopefully, buy it posthaste.

Right there is proof that there are three influences on our kids: their parents, their friends, and television.

Nonetheless, our television-watching setup works, because when my kids are allowed to watch more TV, they get bored. And I feel it's important to let them creatively figure out how to make themselves *not* bored. (This is usually solved by asking children what they plan to *do* to address their boredom, aided by several Mom-inspired pointers.) Besides, being overly restrictive about television in a television-saturated world is like forbidding kids to eat anything with sugar. You know the drill. The cravings start, and they can soon become uncontrollable. My cowriter Karen's son, Emmanuel, once had a playmate whose parents forbade any television in their home. Well, this little girl came over to Karen's house one day, when Mary Poppins was busy dancing with some penguins, and she stood stock-still, absolutely mesmerized as if she'd just been given the world's most soporific drug. Then her mouth dropped open, and she sat down, where she remained motionless, with glazed eyes, until the wind finally blew Mary away again. Karen looked at this poor kid and thought, *You know what, there's got to be a happy medium between too much and this little girl—* who you know will grow up to be in the closet sneaking candy bars while clicking through the HDTV channels until she finds something to float her boat.

What can help with the management of TV-watching is to sit down and watch it with your kids. Sharing my kids' favorite shows with them has become part of our regular time together. In fact, one of my most treasured Friday night activities is pizza-popcorn-TV night. I spend so much time apart from the kids during the week that I love to use that time to reconnect with them.

And it really doesn't have to be some elaborately planned event. They couldn't care less what topping goes on the pizza or what show happens to be on the tube. I kick off my shoes, strip off the war paint, and relax. We laugh together, and we talk about the characters and the story lines, and why the characters are saying something ridiculous or naughty, or doing something even more ridiculous. Even with the most inane animated shows, there's always something to trigger a discussion—about motivation, about the improbability of car- toon physics, about silly catchphrases—if you choose to look at them with a slightly discerning eye. Even better, Casey's and Cole's attention drifts away from the steady diet of *SpongeBob SquarePants*, *The Grim Adventures of Billy and Mandy*, *The Suite Life of Zack and Cody*, and *Hannah Montana*, and on to more interesting topics, like what hap- pened to them at school that day, or whatever else they're thinking about.

It doesn't hurt that my kids really get that I'm on TV and not everyone's mommy *is*. And my brownie points come à la mode when I get to interview people who are big Nickelodeon or Disney stars. (My cool points went through the roof when I

got a powwow with Zack and Cody and an autographed picture to boot.)

Nowadays my kids use the TV just as much for video
games. I allow them to play games on the Xbox and Play-
Station, and they each have a Game Boy and a Nintendo DS.
But it's not any harder to keep the kids in line, since we have
the same rules about video games as we do about television:
No playing till homework is done, and everything in moderation. Frankly, because I've already vetted the games and allow
them to play if they're so inclined, they tend to do it for only a
little while, and then they get bored of whatever game and
move on to the next way to drive me crazy.

Unlike watching TV together, I don't join in when Casey
and Cole are playing video games. I'll admit, they've already
out-techno'd me. They used to ask me how to get to level two
on their Game Boys, and I had a standard reply: "You've got
to be kidding me. I can't even turn the thing on, much less get
you to level two."

Where's that large purple dinosaur when you need him?

please, may i be excused?

WHEN COLE HAD HIS EIGHTH BIRTHDAY PARTY, he was given buckets of toys. A week or so later we were in a store, and what do you think he said?

"Mom, can I have a toy?"

I stopped in my tracks. "What did you just say?" I asked.

"Please, Mom, can I have a toy?"

"Are you out of your mind? You have a room *full* of toys that you haven't even played with yet," I replied as my blood pressure shot well beyond the normal 120 over 70. "Some of them haven't even been unwrapped. No, no, and no—you are not going to get a toy. *No!*"

"But I said *please!*" he protested.

A few days later we were out shopping for some other things. Once again, Cole piped up: "Mom, can I have a toy?"

Okay, so kids are hardwired to beg for toys, but I'm hardwired to say forget about it. This doesn't happen just in toy stores or drugstores or any store that might conceivably have some piece of merchandise that in any way resembles a toy. It often happens after playdates, when some friend or another has X, Y, or Z, which is always more exciting and enticing when someone else's parent has sat up all night with a Phillips screwdriver, cursing the toy manufacturers and whichever droid wrote the instructions in what is supposed to be an instruction manual. Whenever that happens, the question is invariably the same: "Mom, So-and-So has a such-and-such. Can I have one too? Please, can I, please?"

My response is invariably the same too: "What? No, you cannot!"

After which I try my best to explain why the toy in question is not a good toy to have—either it's just like one they might have already, or too expensive, or too inappropriate, or too "I'm not going to buy that overpriced piece of junk that you'll play with for only five minutes before Olivia runs off with it and chews it to shreds."

In my world, toys and manners go together. This is because whenever anyone says the word "toy," my Pavlovian response is to start slobbering with dread at the thought of what toy needs to be purchased that hasn't already been bought for yet another birthday party boy or girl, and how well my kids (well, okay, Cole) will behave at the party. As well as how to manage the inevitable whining that will ensue if the birthday party boy or girl receives more lavish toys than I care to bestow upon my children.

Casey and Cole have social calendars that are more packed than Paris Hilton's. And because they have different friends, they never get invited to the same parties—which invariably means that one party will be on this side of town and the other party will be on the other side of town, and wouldn't you know they both start at two p.m. and end at five p.m.

After I'm handed the invitations and I start wondering how

I'm going to manage the logistics, my next reaction is, *Oh my God, what am I going to get this kid?* And then I say a fervent prayer of thanksgiving for Henny Penny, our local kids' store, which is staffed by teenagers more in sync with what kids want, since they're a lot closer to that age than I am or have been for some time. I never take Casey and Cole in there because I'd surely be broke as a result. Instead, I call the store and tell them how old the birthday child is, what gender, and how much I want to spend, and one of the high school kids who works there after school will pick out an age-appropriate gift and gift wrap it. Then I swing by and pick it up. They haven't failed me yet, and their gift wrapping is impeccable.

The only downside is that my kids will ask what we got the birthday kid and I'll have no idea.

Some parents who don't live close to a Henny Penny are more motivated than I am when it comes to gifts—whenever there's a toy sale on, they buy a bunch of presents for different ages and store them in the gift bag stashed out of reach in the dark recesses of a closet. The trick is to buy things your own kids have no interest in, or to buy an extra toy when your kids are conning you into buying a toy of their own, or, even better, to buy the gift when your own kids are off having a sleepover in another area code.

What drives me crazy about our local birthday bashes is the extravagance of the goodie bags. Casey has returned home from parties with a new purse, or a pair of flip-flops and barrettes, items that cost more than what I spent on the present for the birthday girl. That's sure not going to happen at our house. Our goodie bags are plastic, filled to the very top with candy, and come complete with a card from our dentist stapled to the top.

Which brings me back to the topic of manners. I remember my mother hectoring me to write out thank-you notes, and in retrospect I'm glad she drilled that necessity into me. It's much easier now to insist that my kids get the chore done in a timely fashion. We came up with a brilliant solution, if I do say so myself. We scan a photo from the party into the computer (okay, so Buff does this—I think you've figured out by now that "computer" and "literate" are not two words that are normally strung together in my life); we add a message, such as "Thanks for the gift"; and then the kids sign it. We print them off, drop them in the mail, and away they go!

Manners are incredibly important to me. Rudeness from children really gets under my skin, mainly because I know that if small children are rude, it's because they haven't been properly drilled in social niceties by none other than dear old Mommy and Daddy. I mean, how tough is it to teach kids simple things such as "please," "thank you," "you're welcome," and especially those crucial maxims: "It's rude to stare," and "If you don't have anything nice to say, don't say anything at all."

Neither of which made a dent in Cole the winter I started at CBS in New York and my family was still living in Dallas, where Casey was finishing out the school year. Buff's daughter from his first marriage, the incomparable Tracy Parham, moved in and served as mommy-by-proxy, and still managed to live to tell the tale. When she told me this story, I nearly keeled over!

"Around Christmastime, I had spent the day with the kids and they'd been really good, so as a treat I told them we would get dinner from any restaurant of their choice," she told me. "Surprise! They chose McDonald's.

"I strapped them into their car seats in the back of the minivan and we went to the drive-through window, where we placed our order and then proceeded to the pay window. Now, I have to say that the cashier *was* rather large in size, to the point where she kind of engulfed the small pay window. I gave her the money, we got our food, and we waited there for the cars in front of us to move forward. When, from behind me, a small voice piped up.

"'It's Santa!' Cole said excitedly.

"*Huh?* I wondered, thinking that he might have seen some-one out the window dressed up like Santa. I looked around and didn't see anyone, so I asked him where he saw Santa.

"'The lady!' he replied in a loud voice. 'She's fat like Santa!'

"Bear in mind that the cashier had not closed her window, and could hear every word we were saying. Casey shot Cole a look and told him to be quiet, which, naturally, had precisely the opposite effect.

"'Well, she is!' he pouted.

"Mortified, I glanced over at the cashier, and she looked crushed. I apologized, topped it off with a 'Merry Christmas' (which, given the circumstances, was the exact wrong thing to do), and we moved forward. During the drive home, I explained to Cole how what he had said was not nice and that he needed to watch what he says around people. But my words fell upon deaf ears, as he was too busy chowing down on trans fats to pay any attention to me."

Speaking of meals, where manners are concerned, our biggest battleground is at the dinner table.

See, Buff and I used to have these great visions of the Family

Meal. Manners at the table is the kind of social behavior that's really important to me—especially because Buff travels a lot more than I do, or gets home late from work, and as a result, dinnertime is often just the kids and me. So we started a ritual of Sunday dinner as a Family Meal. And we always try to have Sunday dinner together, the four of us (and Olivia, begging), no matter what.

But we stupidly put too much pressure on ourselves and build up these expectations that dinnertime behavior is going to resemble a Norman Rockwell painting, and what invariably happens is that someone (oh, all right, Cole) scarfs down his food, then gets up to go without another word.

"Sit down, please," I say. "You will not get up and walk around the table. It's rude. And I don't want my children"—okay, this child in particular, as Casey is blessedly well-mannered—"to be rude."

Mumbles and grumbles. Picking at food. He gets up again.

"SIT DOWN!" I yell.

"But I'm finished."

"Well, we aren't. You need to stay till everyone is finished."

You guessed it—in another twenty seconds, he gets up again.

By the end of the meal, I just feel like shouting, *"GET OUT!"*

So then I wonder if my dinnertime frustration comes because I'm putting too much emphasis on this time together—and by doing so I am setting it up to fail, because my expectations are unrealistic—or if my dinnertime frustration comes because manners are so important to me. But then I think, *Is it too much to ask that your kids plant their butts in the seats and then stay there for a scant thirty minutes? If they can plant their carcasses in front of the TV for an hour, why is a half-hour dinner so much more of a struggle?*

Another frustration has to do with not just what the kids are saying but *when* they're saying it. Anyone with a kid over the age of about three has likely lived through the potty talk phase. As the old saying goes, little pitchers have big ears, and my own pitchers have ears the size of an elephant's anytime I cuss or lose it. It's really not funny to hear a three-year-old drop an *F* bomb in front of her teacher, especially when you've just dropped her off at school. (For the record, neither of my kids did that, and neither did I!)

One solution for potty talk is to send kids to the bathroom—as that's where bathroom words belong. Once they know they can say the unmentionables as much as they want, the novelty quickly wears off.

Another technique is the Bad Word Quarter Jar. Whenever anyone says a bad word, he or she must drop a quarter into the jar. The only downside to this method is that sometimes your kids will goad you, deliberately and unmercifully, trying to get you to cuss. They usually succeed too—at least in my house!

The timing of talking is often a problem when it comes to proper phone etiquette, something that I'm a stickler for. My kids can be deeply absorbed in some computer game, or they'll be playing something else, or watching their favorite show on TV, but the minute I pick up the phone, they're all over me. Drives me bonkers!

"Excuse me, you see this thing sticking out of my ear?" I'll tell them. "It's the *telephone*, and I'm talking to someone right now who needs me."

So I tried to teach them the technique of tapping my arm to get my attention, rather than shrieking "MOM, I NEED YOU!" and I ended up with bruises up and down my arms.

Then I tried the "Say 'excuse me' if you need to interrupt me," and the chorus of "EXCUSE ME, EXCUSE ME, EXCUSE ME" played on an endless loop of aggravation.

Of course, I've been at friends' houses where the phone rings, the mom answers it, and the kids shout, "GET OFF THE PHONE NOW!"

I've explained till I'm blue in the face that phone etiquette is crucial, especially in my line of work, which involves constant communication with a wide variety of sources. When I'm on deadline, I don't appreciate having to discuss Teletubbies with the daughter of someone who works from home. I don't need to worry that my messages will be lost or forgotten because a youngster answered the phone and then left me dangling.

Or I'll hear Cole call his friends for playdates, and as soon as someone answers the phone, he'll say loudly, "Who is this?" I tell him that asking "Who is this?" isn't how we speak on the phone, that you introduce yourself, and ask nicely, and say please, and yada, yada, yada.

This takes training and consistency. Which is the hallmark of all manners and etiquette, isn't it?

Okay, so it can take several *years* of training, but you're up to the task, right?

Ginny Farr, a friend of my cowriter Karen's, nips rude

behavior like her daughters' eye-rolling—one of those non-verbal gestures that happens all the time and sends most moms right over the edge—in the bud by sending them off to sit down somewhere to think about, write about, or draw a picture about their thoughts and feelings after an incident.

"We all have to be willing to compromise, and often, for them, that means learning to trust that Mom has more wisdom, and they need to trust in her love for them," Ginny told me. "I'm also willing to admit when I'm wrong, ask for forgiveness, and change directions. I really have to remind myself to listen to them. They're encouraged to express their anger, frustration, or whatever emotion toward me and each other, but with respect and while remembering that the other person has value too. I remind them that our home is a safe and loving place where we can *all* relax and know that we're taken care of. We *all* have to work to make it that way."

Yep, communication, admitting to wrongdoing, and moving on are all hallmarks of the good-enough mother.

I knew the lessons and the years of nagging had rubbed off when an incident happened one afternoon. It had been a long, stressful day at work. My driver was late (my schedule was so crazy, and my start time so early, that I needed to have a car service take me to and from work), he got lost, he was rude, and, worse, I had four big bags in the car. When I got out, he sat on his butt and didn't move so much as a pinkie nail.

"Aren't you going to help me?" I asked, exasperated.

"I'm afraid of your dog," he said with a smirk.

Now, Olivia might like to chew on my only pair of Jimmy

Choos, which I'd bought for 70 percent off, but she's about as threatening as Casey's stuffed chipmunk.

"THIS IS RIDICULOUS!" I shouted as I grabbed the bags, and then I slammed the car door before stomping into the house, where Casey sat, wide-eyed and shocked.

"Mom," she whispered. "He can hear you!"

"You bet," I said loudly. "THAT'S THE POINT."

"Aren't you supposed to give him a tip?" she asked.

"Yeah, here's my tip—buy when stocks are low!"

Once I'd calmed down, I explained to Casey why I'd done what I had. (Trying to explain to an impressionable child why you're screaming at the top of your lungs is perhaps not when you will sound the most rational.) I told her that the driver had been unkind, and I'd just lost it. I told her that we all lose it at some point or another, and use inappropriate manners in the heat of the moment. When that happens, what you do is apologize, and make a mental note that you'll try to do better next time.

Because you know there's going to be a next time.

Another useful tip regarding manners is to use the word "incredible" when you're not sure how to honestly but politely respond to something. "Incredible" can mean good or bad or somewhere in between. But it rarely causes offense, because everyone wants to be thought of as incredible—right?

Or if someone comes to you with a project that is a misshapen mess, or has put on an outfit that clashes so brightly that your eyes hurt, the all-purpose "Wow. I've never seen anything like this before!" says a mouthful without leaving hurt feelings.

So I at least *try* to model good behavior, and I always

explain why it's important to behave respectfully, as Ginny does with her daughters. And how especially important it is to say thank you. I have no trouble telling Casey and Cole, "I did not hear a thank you." One thing I will not condone is having my children grow up with a sense of entitlement—that feeling of "I deserve this, so no thanks are necessary."

No, thank you!

8

chicken nuggets are a food group

THERE ARE THREE WORDS I FEAR MORE THAN ANY other in the English language.

Not: "René, you're fired."

Not: "You're pregnant again." (Though I might faint upon hearing those.)

No, the ones that literally make me quake are: "What's for dinner?"

Dinner is one of those meals that I'm just no good at. I'd like to think it's because I got my day started so early that by the time dinner rolls around, all my creative brain cells are asleep, but the truth is that I never learned to cook. Okay, the *real* truth is that I never had a *desire* to learn how to cook, and I know that I never will.

I'm the type of mom whose favorite words in the kitchen are "cooks in one minute" or "just add water." To me, "scratch" is a great golfer or something you do to an itch.

It's not that I don't *like* to cook. Well, all right, I *don't* like to cook. When it comes to food, the world can be divided into two groups: those who love to cook, read recipes in bed for fun, meander through farmers' markets, obsess about the heft of a chef's knife, and foam at the sight of a Viking Range; and those who don't know how to boil water, and store unused old pots and pans (still in their original wrappings) in the Viking Range they haven't yet figured out how to turn on. Buff falls into the former category, and I am a proud member of the latter.

I don't like waiting for things to be done (too impatient). I don't like cleaning up afterward (enough said). I just don't like to cook!

God bless whoever invented the microwave oven. And prepackaged corn dogs. Don't miss one of the greatest inventions of all time: slice and bake cookies! I mean, how easy can it get? There's no measuring, no dirtying dishes, no flour to leave a trail of mess all over the house, no sugar and butter to cream into a sludgy mess. Heck, a five-year-old can make these kinds of cookies. Turn on the oven, cut the dough into slices (watch the sharp knife if the five-year-old is your sous-chef), and pop those bad boys into the oven for eleven minutes. Voilà. You have fresh, warm cookies that your kids will be so impressed that you made "from scratch."

When it comes to feeding my children, I give myself an F+. The "+" comes from the fact that at least I am trying and my kids are full of energy and growing properly. But when I'm in charge of dinner, they hardly have what I'd call a "balanced diet," unless Tyson chicken nuggets have suddenly found a place on the bottom of the food pyramid. The *F* stands for "Forget about it," because for me, cooking is all about ease and convenience.

Proof of the *F* factor came from my daughter. The other day I was fixing something for dinner and Casey said, "Mom, don't you think we should eat less crap?" Now, when your kid, who never saw a nugget of crap she didn't want to inhale, tells you that, perhaps you really are feeding them too much crap.

I think a lot of my cooking phobia stems from sixth-grade long division. Once I realized that long division—and fractions and measuring and timing and all those pesky other things that have *numerals* in them—had defeated me, I never recuperated. I'm much more of a "broad stroke" kind of person in the kitchen. I mean, really, what's the difference between a quarter cup and a half cup of milk when you're pouring it into a bowl full of packaged pancake mix?

A lot. Trust me, this much I know.

And if I'm being brutally honest, my lack of culinary skills isn't just about math—it somehow has its roots back in what I did and did not learn as a child. I escaped the clutches of puberty without two key skills: how to cook and how to clean. My mother, sensing my complete lack of interest in all things domestic, told me to just make sure I earned enough money one day to hire someone to do the cooking and cleaning *for me*. That became my ultimate goal in high school and college. Not studying hard so I could make meaningful contributions to society. Uh-uh. My goal was getting good grades so I could have a decent career and never have to figure out what lotion works best on dishpan hands.

I suppose my attitude might be a little different now if my mother had been more encouraging. When I was a kid—back in the foodie dark ages, when white bread was a Wonder, arugula was Caligula's kid brother, and margarine was a health food—my mom used to keep a big can of industrial-size Crisco on the stove. Now, if you opened it, don't think you'd actually find *Crisco* in there. That would be too easy. What you'd find instead was the leftover grease from whatever we'd had for dinner the night before. The fried chicken grease, marinating with the hamburger grease, which was complemented by the fish grease with the little flakes of cornmeal garnish. It was beyond disgusting. Yet whenever we needed to lubricate a pan, mom would squish a big spoon into the Crisco can and ladle out a gigantic dollop of that goo, and plop it right into the cast-iron skillet. Then the whole disgusting cycle would start all over again.

It's a wonder my sister and I didn't drop dead at the dinner table.

By the time I got to college, my daily diet wasn't much better. Because I was a runner, I always had a tremendous appetite. But I couldn't afford to fuel it with filet mignon. Instead I became a connoisseur of cheap eats. In fact, it was at college that I perfected the "1001 ways to cook ramen noodles" technique. My diet consisted of said ramen noodles, leftover breakfast from the cafeteria, Little Debbie snacks, and pizza. Somehow I managed to make it through college with my cholesterol levels and my waistline still in check. Ah, those were the days! Of course, now I wouldn't dream of eating like that, but those ramen noodles sure did taste good.

Regardless of my past deficiencies, I suspect a part of my whole issue with the kitchen is a conspiracy engendered by my dearest hubby. He likes to cook—and in our kitchen, there's only room for one top chef. The longer I believe I'm incapable of creating more than toast without a cookbook, the stronger Buff's hold is on his fiefdom.

So I gladly turn most shopping duties over to Buff, who

purchases good, healthy food, grown by real people on real plots of land. I do the snack shopping, where most of that stuff is genetically engineered by real people in real labs, covered head to toe in white suits so as not to come into contact with the dangerous chemicals they're mixing to make "food." As a result, I have become the expert on which kind of Pop-Tarts has more frosting, and whether the lurid orange cheesy Pringles are better than the sour cream and onion variety. Since the kids really *do* need endless piles of snacks for camp and during the school year, I verge on competent on the odd occasion when they actually receive a packet of baby carrots or a piece of fruit for a snack, instead of the usual crunchy blobs of MSG.

Taking the kids food shopping is one of my few recipes whose results are always infallible: It's a disaster. Mine run off in all directions, or turn their noses up at anything that isn't frozen and laden with carcinogenic preservatives, or Cole wants to push the cart, and promptly crashes into the carefully arranged pyramid of canned crushed tomatoes.

Never was my theory about this recipe better proven than the time I went alone to my neighborhood ShopRite after a long day at work. I hadn't changed out of my on-air outfit (for once), and so was uncharacteristically still wearing designer jeans and a white leather coat, with my TV makeup on and my hair done just so. Everyone was so impressed that a real live TV star was buying frozen pizza in their store. I laughingly told the cashier that I was in there all the time, but dressed down so much that they never recognized me.

Well, a week later I was back in the store, clad in my usual afternoon outfit of grungy sweats, with my hair squashed under a baseball cap, face scrubbed clean, fake eyelashes nowhere in sight, and, oh yeah, paint splattered all over my sandal-clad feet (I'd been refinishing a chair I'd found on the street). Naturally, both kids were with me, and, just as naturally, the kids were squabbling with each other and with me. This time the squabble centered on the devastatingly important topic of—what else?—who got to push the cart.

Cole won the coin toss, and because he was busy being Cole, he was messing around. I told him, the first time he hits me with that thing, it's mine. You guessed it, thirty seconds later he ran over my heels. Wincing in agony, I grabbed the cart, and he started to scream. At which point the same people who a week ago had thought I was the epitome of glamour were now ready to call child protective services because my son was having a meltdown in the cereal aisle.

But in supermarkets I have zilch problem saying no to my kids. If Casey wants Fruit by the Foot and Cole wants Fruit Gushers and then they want to throw one more box of some high-fructose-corn-syrup-drenched thing into the cart, I am perfectly capable of removing it and ignoring the inevitable whining that ensues. Even I have my limits!

Just when you think you've got the whole snack thing under control, though, one of your kids will come home after a playdate/gorge-fest at one of their friends' houses, and all they can talk about is what they've been deprived of *chez nous*. I mean, how was I supposed to know that waffle fries tasted so good? Or that yogurt comes in little containers with Oreos or granola on top? I tell ya, some moms have a lot of nerve, raising the bar for the rest of us, who wouldn't know a waffle cut from a watermelon smoothie.

My neighbor was over the other day, and after a nice visit she looked at her watch and said that she had to leave because she had to go brown some hamburger meat and onions for her famous homemade spaghetti sauce. I was exhausted just listening to her. Did I tell her that the only time I ever found myself browning meat was for tacos or Hamburger Helper? No, I did not.

But I try my best. Whether I'm buying junk or serving it, I still pride myself on my hypocrisy. I'm always discussing the importance of a balanced meal with my kids, and trying to fit in minilectures about how growing bodies need to have protein and complex carbohydrates, to build muscles and to have energy. They don't want to turn out to be the class weaklings, do they?

Then the inevitable "eat your vegetables" lesson starts. I tell them about the essential nutrients and brain food that can be found only in vegetables and fruit. And if that doesn't work, I pull out the old standby—the "you'll get constipated if you don't eat your vegetables" lecture. Trust me, no one at the Parham estate wants poop problems.

Sometimes there is still balking, usually from Casey.

Only one response works: "This is not a *diner*, this is your *dinner*," I'll tell her.

"But, Mommy, you know I don't like corn," she'll protest.

"Well, you have to eat one bite," I calmly reply. "You may not like it, but it's good for you and you have to have it. And if you don't, you're not going to eat another thing tonight."

Meaning no dessert—which is an even more powerful incentive than constipation.

So, Casey, my good girl, will eat her one bite of corn. And

then I won't serve it for a while because it's not good to force kids to eat foods they loathe (liver, anyone?) just because those foods are full of vitamins and fiber. Instead, I can resort to my old standbys of broccoli, carrots, and cauliflower. Yes, they're all served with fattening ranch dressing, but it helps my kids eat the good stuff, along with my tried-and-true favorites, such as tacos.

I know what I can do, and do well—which is why we often have breakfast for dinner (something nutritious, such as pancakes mixed from the box) at least once a week. One of these "breakfast for dinner" meals includes a recipe from a friend, and the dish is now known as my famous "mancakes," mini-pancakes laced with chocolate chips and smothered in whipped cream (from the can).

Mancakes are one of the few things I actually can cook without burning. Yes, I can cook a mean mancake after years of experimenting with just *how much* water to add to the "just add water" pancake mix. And get this—I don't even need a measuring cup anymore! (One less thing to clean up.) The mancakes are a special treat in my household, one doled out in moderation, because both of my kids have a dangerous weakness for sweets. At least Casey will come downstairs and ask if she can have something sweet to eat. Cole will go right to the pantry and merrily help himself. It doesn't matter where I hide the candy. That boy has a sixth sense: He's the candy-sniffer. If it has sugar, he's going to find it.

This can be a bit of a dilemma when it's snack time after school. Kids need nutritious food to fill the gap between schooltime and dinnertime. Something with the right balance of protein and complex carbohydrates. Like peanut butter on whole-grain bread. Or carrot sticks and hummus.

Not Cole's favorite—a marshmallow sandwich.

"But, Mom," he protests. "It's *whole wheat* bread!"

One way I indulge Casey's sweet tooth is to have her help me when I bake. (Cole's only interest is in licking the bowl.) Casey's pretty good at cracking eggs and helping to mix, and Cole is really good at cracking anything and making a mess. But clearly something is rubbing off, as my letting them be hands-on means that when they come into the kitchen, announcing that they're hungry, and I tell them to make themselves something to eat, they will.

That is, after I've steered Cole away from the candy stash.

Still, I have a ways to go. Last time I told Casey I was in the mood to make some brownies, she looked at me and, without batting an eye, said, "Are they going to come from a box?"

I laughed out loud because, heck yeah, they were going to come from a box. I am a box-brownie connoisseur!

She was, thankfully, truly impressed once I figured out how to make a cake in the microwave oven. This is the world's best tip for baking phobics like me. You get yourself a silicone pan and you dump everything in there and mix it around for a minute, and then you put it in the microwave for ten minutes, and like magic you've got yourself a cake. Plus it pops right out of the silicone pan. We add all sorts of sprinkles, and the kids get a thrill out of making a mess with them, and we're all happy.

For me, cooking isn't so much about the outcome as it is about the *process*. Having a perfectly frosted, crumb-free cake isn't important. Having a cake that's good enough because it was made to please, is.

Believe me, we've had enough disasters. Some earlier

cake attempts were mush. Others were a crumbly horrid mess, but the cakes didn't have to look perfect. They just had to taste good.

Whether it's from box, freezer, or jar, Casey and Cole know that food in my kitchen has been prepared with love.

Which is the tastiest ingredient of all.

all roads lead to math

THE THIRD GRADE ALMOST KILLED ME.

Not *my* third grade experience, mind you, but my kids'. Once I saw their homework—the work sheets covered in figures and fractions—my heart started to thump and my head began to swim. I felt as if I were being haunted by the Ghost of Homework Past.

Since I'm a professional journalist, it may not come as a surprise that I was (and still am) a voracious reader, of anything from the classics to my beloved collection of Nancy Drew books, and I was a more-than-passable English student in school. My friends thought I was nuts, because I *liked* to write book reports and keep up with summer reading lists.

But don't get me started on math.

I hated math.

If you don't believe me, ask Mr. McCullough, my much-maligned high school math teacher, because I wore out my britches and three desks in his class, one for each year I was there, endlessly failing to understand just what the heck algebra was and why on earth I was plagued enough to have to think about it. Never did the poor guy see any improvement in my algebra skills or in my disposition in (not) dealing with them.

By the time Casey started school, I had had many long years of freedom from figures. Long, lovely years devoid of the need to count anything more taxing than calories.

Which is why I broke into a cold sweat when Casey came home from third grade one fine day and, good girl that she is, sat down with an apple and a cookie and a glass of milk, spread out her homework, and then dropped the bomb.

She needed help with fractions.

Fractions? *FRACTIONS!* Lord have mercy, there were twenty years of cobwebs filling the minuscule area of gray matter that ever dealt with fractions. Any ability to understand fractions hadn't been replaced by just cobwebs, but by partying, glasses of wine, childbirth, early morning wake-up calls, and trying to keep Cole from destroying the house. My fraction-capable brain cells—all three and three quarters of them—had long been lost in the Bermuda Triangle of life's priorities.

Of course I couldn't tell any of this to Casey, lest she think her mother a completely incompetent booby. But seriously, how on earth do you explain math to an impressionable child when you don't get it yourself? Or how do you explain that the mere thought of adding anything with a number higher than the ten fingers on my hands triggers the kind of anxiety that cannot be assuaged with my usual "I Don't Care" mantra?

See, a good-enough mother knows she's not perfect, that she's a normal bundle of anxieties and inadequacies and that she has some really finely honed skills and some boneheaded tendencies that usually result in belly flops or fallen soufflés. In other words: She's human.

But I don't want my children to think that I can't succeed at something *if I really put my mind to it.* Not that I'd expect to come out a gold-medal winner, but I'd expect to do the best I could and that that would be good enough. Just as crucial: They need to know that they'll succeed as well, *if they put their minds to it.* It's also crucial for them to learn that if they don't succeed, they need to try another tactic to get the goal accomplished.

Teaching these things to children is very hard to do when you're convinced you're going to fail. I feel as dizzy when confronted with math homework now as I did whenever Mr. McCullough breezily informed the class that he was springing a pop quiz on us. I knew I would fail then—and I did. Now whenever I see the figures swimming on the sheet of math homework, I fear I will fail again, even if I really put my mind to it. Moreover, each time I supervise Casey's doing the equations, I wonder if perhaps this might be the one time when I really and truly will be revealed to be a phony, revealed as a mom who *can't* deal with anything and everything, and I will disappoint my children.

As a result, it takes an awful lot of energy for me to put on a cheery face when math homework appears out of the backpacks. I take deep breaths and tell myself that if an eight-year-old can be expected to solve the problems, then a forty-four-year-old mother can at least try to do the same.

So when Casey first needed help with fractions, I hauled out the measuring cups in the kitchen, and tried to figure out how much one half plus three quarters equals. I cracked open a Diet Coke—fervently wishing either that it would turn into a stiff vodka or that my financial-whiz husband would magically appear home early from work—and tried to keep my voice steady as I surveyed Casey's fraction work sheet.

"See, Mommy," my sweet Casey said, pointing to some figures. "I don't know how to multiply the fractions, or divide the fractions. Can you help me?"

Multiply the fractions? *Divide* the fractions? Ugh—I couldn't even show her how to *add* the fractions. And here's the kicker . . . she had to show her work!

After she went to bed that night, I had a good long soak in the tub, trying to convince myself that a good-enough mother knows enough to look at the bright side. Diagram a sentence, done. Conjugate verbs, I'm there. Bring store-bought cupcakes to class, no problem. I negotiated an uneasy truce with myself, concentrating on my strengths and trying my utmost not to admit that there are still some things I will always suck at. Like fractions.

Wouldn't you know, just when I was starting to believe I might be able to figure out the dreaded fractions, Casey came home one other fine day with a new way to strike terror into my heart.

That's right, my old nemesis: long division.

And now Cole is going through the third grade, so out come the frantic calculations again. I know it's going to be a whole lot more difficult, not only because geometry is looming and there's no way I'm ever going to figure that stuff out, but also because Casey is good at sitting down to do her homework, while her dearest brother never saw an assignment he didn't want to wiggle out of.

To be honest, one of the reasons our rule about homework is "Get it done ASAP" is so I can look forward to a nice dinner and an evening devoid of fractions.

But despite my best efforts, back when Cole was in second grade, nothing could stop a certain something from happening that felt like a hot poker to the gut.

That certain something was a note from the teacher.

And not just any note, nor just any teacher.

This was a note from Mrs. Henry.

The mere sound of Mrs. Henry's voice was guaranteed to send me into paroxysms of terror. And now she'd sent a note home with Cole. Hands trembling, I carefully plucked the large green Post-it off Cole's spelling homework.

I think we need to have a conference at your earliest convenience, it read.

My knees practically buckled.

After I quizzed my second-born about the reason for the note, he finally managed to stammer that, well, okay, maybe he *did* have a homework problem. One that went beyond a math-incompetent mother.

And then there was the matter of the bass. It seemed that he'd tied his shoelaces together and had been bunny-hopping around the music room, one of his preferred schooltime activities, and, as usual, had lost his balance. While toppling over, he'd nearly busted the school's upright bass. A bass that cost upward of a cool thousand bucks. That's a whole lot of weeks of a five-dollar allowance to pay off that debt, I managed to explain to Cole, whose eyes only got bigger and rounder as the specter of NO ALLOWANCE UNTIL HE WAS TWELVE finally wove its way into the dense thicket of his gray matter.

But back to homework. The real pisser was that that night I'd arrived home at seven thirty p.m., after leaving the house at four a.m., to find Buff with his feet nonchalantly propped up on the desk while the kids were running wild. Seriously. Casey was behaving nearly normally (for her), but Cole had placed Scotch tape over his mouth and eyes and was navigating the spiral staircase in a pair of slippery socks. For crying out loud, the only thing missing was a knife between his lips!

And when I tried to ask Buff in a calm voice if the homework had been done, his reply was: "They told me it was."

At which point I began to lose what little mind I had left. "Buff," I said in what I hoped was a more-than-stern-get-your-damn-feet-down-off-the-desk-and-listen voice. "You cannot *ask* if the homework is done. You have to *check* it—much the way our government asks rogue nations if they have nuclear weapons, and even then the CIA *still* has to verify. If there's one thing you ought to know by now, it's that you can never take your own children's word at face value whenever the topic is *homework*."

Because Buff is not a good-enough mother like yours truly, he gave me his typical response to the aforementioned more-than-stern-get-your-damn-feet-down-off-the-desk-and-listen voice.

He shrugged.

So I schlepped over to the kids' backpacks to fish for the homework. I already knew what I would find: homework so incomplete it would undoubtedly receive an I for a grade. Casey hadn't done her sketch of the moon, which had been her assignment for the previous three heavily overcast days, but her excuse was at least valid—the clouds *had* gotten in her way.

Cole couldn't blame his undone spelling list on the clouds.

Worse, stuck to his paper was the dreaded note from the teacher.

I'm afraid to say that my response was not pretty.

Buff finally removed his tootsies from the desk, and went stomping off in search of his favorite loungewear. Never mind that his favorite loungewear is a ratty velour sweat suit. Buff knew he'd messed up. The week before, I'd explained to him (for the umpteenth time) that if Cole got bad reports from school, or didn't finish his homework, the TV had to stay off. Naturally, at the time, Buff had been in complete and total agreement with me.

But tonight, when the buck had stopped with Buff, he'd totally dropped the ball. He hadn't even glanced at the homework—if he had, he'd have seen the dreaded note.

And Cole would not have already consumed several hours of television he'd known he wasn't supposed to be watching.

Now, I need to make it clear that when I examine the homework, I don't literally correct my kids' mistakes. If I see a lot of errors, however, I'll sit down with them and make some helpful suggestions for corrections and gently explain what might have been confusing or done too quickly. Casey and Cole know that I never make excuses for them if their home-work hasn't been done properly. (Of course, I never, ever do the fractions, and wouldn't even if I knew how!)

That's because I'm busy placing a certain ratty velour sweat suit on a makeshift funeral pyre in the backyard.

Seriously, though, it is easier to deal with the homework when there's a routine. Children thrive on a regular schedule, and I started small with Casey and Cole. They get home from school, put down their backpacks (okay, fling them down with a sigh and a thump is more like it), have a snack, decompress for a while, and then they know it's time for homework. It's especially crucial to set up a schedule similar to this one (and it can be pushed back till after dinner if there are after-school activities) when kids are young, because it instills in them the knowledge that homework is a given, and that it must be done. The deeper the homework habit is entrenched, the easier homework will be to manage when kids reach middle and high school and the pressures and demands of homework become far more intense.

One problem I need to stay on top of is that Cole wants to do the homework only for subjects he likes. Getting him to do the rest can degenerate into a battle. He has a real aptitude for math, which delights me because I have fewer fractions to worry about, but his spelling and reading assignments can be tough. I explain to him that grown-ups often have to deal with the same situation at work. For instance, I sometimes have to report on something I'm not totally passionate about, but I need to do it with the same level of enthusiasm and professionalism as I would for a topic I'm thrilled by. He understands that, of course, but it doesn't make the grumbling any less annoying!

I really am strict about no TV or computer time until the homework is done and I've inspected it. But when the weather is nice, I don't insist that Casey and Cole do their homework the minute they walk in the door after school. In fact, I kick them right back out again, to go play in the big backyard for an hour or so before coming back in to tackle the work. That's what the yard is there for, and after being cooped up in classes all day, it does their bodies (and minds) good to get out and run around and scream and shout and throw some balls with Olivia.

This is something I learned from my mother. Since we

grew up in California, where the weather was usually lovely, Mom insisted that we get our homework done as quickly as possible, so my sister and I had the rest of the afternoon to play outside with our friends, or hang out, or read, or drive our mother crazy.

One thing that drives *this* mother crazy is school projects. I don't mind helping Casey and Cole put things together once they've conceptualized the project, but I do mind that other parents are so determined to impress the teacher that they end up doing all the work themselves. (You know, decorating the projects with Sistine Chapel–worthy paintings, hand-looming a blanket, building a Noah's ark out of toothpicks and cedar shavings, tatting lace, or cultivating a few bonsai atop a miniature lily pond stocked with baby koi.)

For a Valentine's Day project last year, Casey needed to decorate a shoe box to hold her valentine cards. We found a terrific box and she and I got this ridiculous idea of covering the entire box in crepe paper. After spending the next five hours covering a scant quarter of the box, I asked myself for the umpteenth time why we couldn't have come up with a better way. (I loved doing the project together, but, well, five hours with crepe paper is about four too many.)

Luckily, I thought, Cole only had to do a shoe-box lunch for his Valentine's Day project. Shoe-box lunches sound simple, but they often aren't. Each student picks a name of a classmate out of a hat, and then has to bring in either a shoe-box or a metal lunch box decorated with something the classmate likes, along with his or her favorite food and drink tucked inside.

Cole's recipient was a soccer player, so I went online to

buy a soccer-themed lunch box. Sounds easy, right? Wrong. Cole told me about this Valentine's Day project only three days before it was due (and, naturally, over the weekend), so I had to pay for extra shipping to get the specific lunch box in time. A four-dollar lunch box ended up costing forty.

Don't even get me started on the dreaded dioramas. My heart usually sinks when I hear that one has been assigned, not only because by the time I get home from work my brain cells either are on strike or are fried to a crisp—and I often find it hard to help Cole come up with something fanciful and complicated at a moment's notice—but also because this assignment can degenerate into a snarky competition among the parents, each trying to outdo the other with the sophistication of their conceptualizing and the rarity of the materials. There's no way I can compete with the parents who have time to comb eBay for one-of-a-kind items—such as miniature Hummers or porcelain dolls with dresses handcrafted by Lithuanian seamstresses—in order to build perfect, museum-quality dioramas.

Plus, I am adamant that I will *not* do all of my kids' work for them.

Nor, truth be told, do I want to. Children need to know that the power of their own imagination is far more potent and fascinating than any designer-labeled item their parents can scrounge around for or score for them. They should be dreaming up ideas for their dioramas on their own, to be built with their own hands from materials they can easily procure on a limited budget (if that). But this becomes next to impossible when their projects are judged against the well-financed, architecturally blueprinted projects created by parents. I don't want my children to feel inadequate when their lovingly home-made projects are deemed inferior because the rules of the competition are unfairly rigged against them, but I have as yet been unable to convince the teachers to state unequivocally that parental guidance and hands-on assistance is forbidden.

So when Cole once "forgot" to tell me he had to do a dreaded diorama of a fairy tale (he'd chosen *Jack and the Beanstalk*), it nearly did me in.

Off we drove to the local supersize drugstore, my mind racing with ideas of how to cram a little Jack and a giant Giant into the shoe box of the dreaded diorama as I made Cole think aloud about ideas. The only thing at the store that could possibly pose as Jack was a small green soldier, but he was holding a machine gun. I shuddered and put him back on the shelf. Then after another twenty minutes of searching, we found another character, but he was too big to be Jack, so we decided he'd be a good giant. After more fruitless searching, it was back to the machine-gun-toting soldier.

"Mommy, it's fine," Cole said. "Let's just get something green to be the bean stalk."

Right. When Buff got home, he heard the entire story, took one look at my face, and then went out into the backyard with an anxious Cole and dug up a piece of turf with an enormous weed growing in it. When Cole saw that, he was thrilled, and knew exactly what to do with it.

Voilà, the dreaded diorama—a gun-wielding psycho Jack, a large stuffed Giant, and a weed for a bean stalk. And it cost only a couple of bucks. It looked, well, *unique*. Cole was thrilled that both his parents had helped him construct it—but more important, he learned that no matter what his diorama looked like in comparison to the psycho-free shoe boxes of his classmates, he'd done most of it himself. He was proud of his efforts and he knew *we* were proud of it.

Fortunately, the dreaded dioramas don't get assigned all that often, but daily homework does. I know there's a lot of vociferous debate about kids being given endless hours of sometimes numbingly repetitious busywork and homework, but in our school district I don't find Casey and Cole overburdened—yet. Casey doesn't mind doing homework—in fact, she likes it. She's an even more voracious reader than I was at her age. Whenever I take her to a bookstore, she wants to move in. Cole, on the other hand, wants to buy books only if they come with a toy. Motivating him to get the homework done, or to read for pleasure, is much more of a struggle. I'm riding him like the Romans rode Spartacus.

Which is why I was so surprised one night when I was relaxing with the kids and Casey handed me her notebook to sign. I was full of pride as I went over the things she'd accomplished, but my bubble quickly burst when I saw an item she was supposed to bring to school. A gallon.

A gallon of *what*? Milk? Spit? Paint? I had no idea. Worse, Casey didn't either. She was nearly in tears, since she so rarely forgets anything, and was becoming increasingly upset at the thought of not fulfilling an assignment. Normally, of course, I would have made her suffer the consequences of her forgetfulness, but a good-enough mother knows when to forgive a legitimate oversight and deal with it as best she can on the spur of the moment.

So although both of us were half-asleep, we spent the next

half hour searching the house until we realized we didn't even have a gallon. Of *anything*.

Casey's tears began to flow in earnest, and I kissed them away and told her to go to sleep and not to worry. Although she knew the rule—that she is responsible for reading all the notes in her backpack and has to face the consequences if something doesn't get done—in this case I would make an exception because she'd made a genuinely honest mistake.

A good-enough mother always knows when to bend the rules.

The only thing I could find on my way out the door at 4:10 the next morning was a half-filled half-gallon carton of skim milk. So, what did I do? Dumped out the milk (mercifully there was another half gallon in the fridge), rinsed the carton three times, and compromised. A half gallon was better than none.

There. Crisis averted.

Just don't ask me to add one half and three quarters.

you're not the boss of me!

WHEN I WAS PREGNANT WITH COLE, I WAS convinced that I would never love any baby as much as I loved Casey, my sweet little cupcake. Everyone, especially parents of more than one child, told me, "Oh, yes, you *will* love them both like crazy—but in different ways."

I wasn't placated until I held Cole in my arms for the first time—noticing that he was already rooting around for the breast—and realized that all these other parents were right, of course. Having two is like watching the doors of your heart get flung open, and what you thought had room for only one now has more than enough room for two. How this magical phenomenon happens, and *why* it happens, is something I can't answer. Casey and Cole are so utterly unalike—Casey is a fragile flower and Cole is a tough nut (and a mini-me)—but my love for each isn't unalike.

But how I deal with them is unalike!

I want to go on record as saying I'm lucky that my kids don't fight all that much, relatively speaking. Of course they argue and bicker and get in each other's hair, sometimes with more vehemence than I care to hear, but when I see what goes on in some of their playmates' homes, I say yet another prayer of thanksgiving that I've been blessed with my kids.

Sibling rivalry is something I lived through, as I grew up with a sister twenty-two months younger than I was. We got along well enough until about the fourth grade, when I grew to regard her as a real pill and a serious impediment to an enjoyable life. See, my mother did something that in retrospect worsened the situation (but of course at the time, she didn't have a choice because we couldn't afford babysitters). After school and on weekends, Mom made me take Tracy with me wherever I went. There was no discussion or explanation— I was merely ordered to watch her. When I was six it wasn't so much of a problem having Tracy tag along, but by the time I was eight or nine, it certainly was. I thought it was blatantly unfair that I had to have my annoying little sister intruding on what I wanted to do with my friends all the time, solely because my mother said I had to do it. (Believe me, it wasn't because I was such a great babysitter—Mom just wanted Tracy to go with me because I was far more social.)

I know this situation, so typical with most of my peers, unwittingly fostered a deep resentment and sibling rivalry, one that I doubt would have been so strong if Tracy had not been forced to be in my face all the time. And it was no better for her—she wasn't as loud or as outgoing as I was, and she certainly didn't want to tag along with me any more than I wanted her there.

Once I had two children, I made a conscious decision not to force them to play together. Because I don't force it, Casey and Cole often want to play together. The decision becomes their choice, and as a result, they get along much better.

I'm sure this will change once those teenage hormones kick in (although I can hope that it won't), but for now, Casey and Cole are not stuck with each other, they're stuck *on* each other. They like playing together, whether outside in the yard or inside with the PlayStation. They play together much more than they fight. They'll hole up in each other's bedrooms and invent games and put on shows. Sometimes they'll spend weeks sleeping in each other's rooms, sharing secrets with only each other.

I don't take it personally when my kids shut me out. In fact, a good-enough mother is grateful that her children are happy to discuss things with their siblings—especially as she hopes that the exchange of confidences will continue throughout their adult lives.

Part of what helps Casey and Cole get along is that they possess diametrically opposed interests and temperaments. I believe these marked differences make it much easier for them to look out for each other and truly love each other. They aren't in constant competition, and they don't complain about having to share toys, or about who got a bigger one, or about being compared because one could do something before the other one could master it. They don't step on each other's toes.

Naturally, I have wondered what life on the Parham estate might have been like if Casey and Cole had been more like peas in a pod. Some of my friends have described their children this way, and have told me of the seemingly inevitable rivalries that have wreaked havoc on their families. Sometimes children just do not get along; you can't force people who have extremely divergent interests or personalities to be crazy about each other. Family members may just inherently be like the same magnetic polarity—repelling each other instead of attracting.

If that happens, moms might want to encourage each child to find something that he or she is really good at and to develop that skill—something like art, writing, or sports. That way you can help foster each child's individuality, and you can try to minimize some of the inevitable comparisons, since the last thing you want to do is deliberately play siblings off each other. I know I'm guilty of falling into the comparison trap, and I gave myself a stern talking-to the day I heard "Why can't you be more like your sister?" come tripping out of my mouth. It was something I'd hated hearing as a child and had sworn I'd never say to my own children.

Or sometimes parents unwittingly play favorites, which can embitter or shut down children who feel cast off or less loved. Trust me on this—every mom of siblings knows that children have eagle-eyed X-ray vision when it comes to ensuring that they each get exactly the same thing and that no one is getting more than his or her fair share, whether a scoop of ice cream, a serving of french fries, a new outfit, a computer game, or attention from Mom. Otherwise, the chorus of "It's not fair!" can be deafening.

One time, my little cherubs decided to spend the afternoon digging up all my tomato plants, wetting down the expensive topsoil before throwing the stinking mess all over the planters and the patio. When I discovered the damage, and after I was finished screaming about it, I ordered them to clean it up.

Casey began to dutifully tackle her mess. Cole pushed his around. This meant, of course, that instead of watching what they were doing and quickly getting it done, they were too busy watching each other to make sure that each was doing exactly the very same iota of (non) work as the other one.

"But, Mom," both of them yelled. *"It's not fair!"*

When I hear the "It's not fair" chorus, I often think of the story my television agent, Henry, told me about his three children and their two-week Greek vacation. At the time of this vacation his daughter, Sally, was fifteen, his son Jared was fourteen, and his son Corey was eleven.

"Normally, the kids get along really well," Henry told me, "so they didn't mind sharing a room at all. Sally and Jared are good friends, and Corey was thrilled to be hanging with his teenage siblings—something that never happens at home.

"All was fine until night thirteen, when Sally banged on our door, telling us that she couldn't take it anymore, and that she didn't understand why she couldn't have her own room. I asked her what was going on, and she said, 'Why can't they lift the toilet seat? Every time I walk into the bathroom, there's pee on the seat. And when we're in our room at night, the boys start fighting and farting and it just goes on and on.

"'Just what the hell is wrong with them?' she asked.

"Cut to the next night when we were all sitting at dinner for our last meal in Greece, and I was busy basking in the glory of a very successful family bonding experience. So I was thanking the kids for their good cheer (okay, I was lying) and attitude, and I was saying they deserved some recognition for their participation in making this a great trip.

"'I should receive special recognition for my participation,' said Jared, 'since I wore only two pairs of underwear the whole time!'

"Revolted, I asked him how that was possible, and he replied that he'd brought along his two favorite pairs of boxers, and each night he would wash one of them in the sink before going to bed.

"'THIS IS WHAT I'M TALKING ABOUT!' yelled Sally. 'I go in to brush my teeth, only to find a pair of my brother's underwear floating around in the sink. You think that's fair? *It's not fair!*'"

Yep, I have so much to look forward to! How many times do we wonder if the siblings who get along so well at eight and ten will try to tear each other's hair out at sixteen and fourteen. Or if they'll move away after college and never want to see their siblings if they can possibly help it?

What I try to do in the meantime is remain hypervigilant, as Cole tends to be more outwardly needy due to his natural exuberance, and Casey is so easygoing and eager to please that it can sometimes be just a little too easy to breeze over anything that might be troubling her deep inside. I know I've been guilty of this too—paying too much attention to Cole because he's so obvious about what's going on, while Casey tends to internalize. They both need me, in different ways, and I make sure that I spend as much time alone with each of them as I possibly can.

What really pleases me is that Casey benefits from Cole's adventurousness, and he learns from her steadiness. He lends her a bit of his joie de vivre, and she thankfully contributes a bit of stability. Isn't it true that free spirits can blossom only when they're secure in the steadiness around them? If Cole had an older sibling who was as much of a free spirit as he is, I can't help but wonder if that would create too much of a competitive situation and cause him to act out in an unpredictable manner.

Somehow, knowing Cole as well as I do, I kind of doubt it! Example: Cole decided he had to have Heelys—you know, those shoes with the small wheels housed in the heels that have given rise to countless mothers risking heart failure while watching their kids zoom off down their driveways. I don't know if Cole wanted them because his friends had them or because he wanted the opportunity to break his neck, but after weeks of nagging, his father gave in and got him the dang things, which Cole loves dearly and wears all the time. So far, he's managed to remain upright.

Casey surprised me when she asked for a pair too. Now, keep in mind that Casey is not a real daredevil like Cole. Did she want them because she really was interested in wearing them, or did she simply need to have the same thing her brother had (the hallmark of all siblings)?

I certainly wasn't about to discourage any adventurousness in Casey, so I bought her a pair. The last thing you ever want to do for a child with a timid or shy streak is plant any seeds of doubt in her mind—you know, the "Don't climb up the ladder because you might fall down" sort of thing. It *can* be hard to squelch your instinct to hover around or be over-protective of a child who needs more protection than a rough-and-tumble sibling—but these are often the kids who blossom the most when you give them the benefit of the doubt and encourage them to be a little bit more adventurous. They won't know unless they try. If they do their best, it's the best they can do.

Still, as Casey and Cole are so very different—Casey is a rule maker and Cole is a rule breaker—this can cause some clashes. Casey makes the rules, and Cole just goes ahead and breaks them. And this can be tough, since it seems as if that's his primary motivation in life. In response, I don't want Casey to become a snitch, which can be a real temptation for her, especially when Cole is being deliberately naughty. Casey's behavior is motivated by her own strict, internal moral code. When she knows there's a rule, and that the rule is right, she wants that rule to be respected. And she's often fearful that something really wrong is being perpetrated—so she'll tattle on the wrongdoer.

As a parent, you want kids to figure things out on their own (as long as they're not doing something dangerous or engaging in flagrant rule-breaking), but you also know that you need to be alerted when something dangerous is going down. It can be quite tricky to know the difference between merely telling on someone and reporting about something important, such as an incident of hitting or cruelty. I wish I had some universal answer to that, because tattling is annoying— but sometimes it needs to be done. You can't say today that tattling is okay, and say tomorrow that it's wrong.

When the kids come squawking to me about an incident that does not involve bleeding or a lump on the head, an incident that does not involve immediate parental intervention, my response is simple: "Work it out."

Kids need to learn how to problem-solve on their own. They have to learn to share. They have to learn to control their moods. They can't do this if you swoop in every time there's bickering, fighting, or less than exemplary behavior.

What I sometimes think about, particularly because a lot of this is out of my control, is how the sweetest, most loving and considerate little girls can suddenly morph into bossy little brats. I see the Mean Girl Syndrome happening to some of my daughter's schoolmates, who are on the cusp of teendom. And it ain't pretty—some of those girls are *nasty*. What worries me is that Casey is docile and eager to please, and I don't want her getting caught up in the popularity dramas that are really just emotional abuse and bullying cloaked in a veneer of surface niceness.

Moms who parent children as hypersensitive as Casey is will also relate to how carefully I need to tread when she takes rivalries too seriously, and loses it emotionally. It's hard to know when to push and when to stand back.

Example: We were on a family vacation and decided to play a game of croquet, something we all love. As we set up the course, Casey listened carefully to my instructions, and tried hard to win. (Cole, not surprisingly, whacked the ball every which way, and had a grand old time doing so.) But at the end of the game, Casey collapsed into a ball of tears. I sent Buff and Cole down the road to get some ice cream, and I sat down with her on a bench, hugging her close and letting her weep for a few minutes.

"Why are you crying?" I gently asked her. I never want her to think of me as insensitive and uncaring, or to think that I don't love her, but I do know that at the same time she needs to toughen up a little bit, and she has to try to keep her over-reactions in check.

"Because I didn't win," she eventually sputtered. "Cole beat me."

"But it's just a game, Casey," I told her. "One that we've played before and will play again. You have to understand that you are almost ten years old and cannot be crying over a game of croquet. Especially when four people played and only one can be the winner. Besides, no one wants to play with someone who wins all the time. Or someone who's a sore loser. Right?"

She cried a little bit more, then dried her tears, and we kept on talking about how the *playing* is what counts, not the outcome.

Cole, on the other hand, doesn't care so much whether he wins or loses, as long as he has fun and can play his way. What he cares more about is being the boss. No nasty girls will ever dare tell him his shirt clashes with his pants, or he has a funny haircut, or his dimples are funky. Uh-uh. I'd like to see them try!

Speaking of bossy, get this. There I was in the bathroom, trying to get dressed one morning last summer. The kids were like raw nerves because they'd been up late the night before (that being, of course, the summer of TV and sugar). Suddenly I heard screaming. Now, here I was, feeling like giving them the usual lesson about how to treat people how you want to be treated, even though the sound of their screaming was like nails being dragged slowly down a chalkboard.

But instead of calmly going to find out what was causing the screaming, a "WHAT THE HELL IS GOING ON?" exploded out of my mouth before I could stop it.

In trotted Casey, her eyes swimming. "Cole called me stupid," she said. "Three times! And he hit me!"

My head started to spin, because in our house we are not about calling people names; we're not about using our hands to hit. Hitting is for people who can't use their words, and calling anyone names is for people who can't use their words well.

What was my response? "GO GET COLE!"

A few minutes went by. No Cole. Which, naturally, got me

even more pissed off. I stomped out of the bathroom in search of my son, only to find him merrily playing a game on his computer.

"Didn't Casey tell you to come see me?" I asked.

"Yeah," he replied, without taking his eyes off the screen.

"Well, then, why didn't you come in?"

"I was closing this out," he said.

"Hold it right there," I said, snatching the controller from his grasp. "When Casey says, 'Mom wants you,' you stop what you're doing right that minute, I don't care if you're playing something. Stop right now and come see me."

Sighing and moaning with the weight of the world on his shoulders, he dragged himself into my room, where Casey was already waiting.

"Okay," I said in my best (hopeless) imitation of Judge Judy. "What happened? Why was there so much screaming?"

"He took my bookmark," Casey said.

"It's not your bookmark," Cole protested.

"Great," I said. "I don't know whose bookmark it is. It doesn't have a name tag on it, and I don't care—that's not the point. The point is, there's no hitting in this house. And there's no name-calling. Did you call Casey stupid?"

"Well, she *can* act stupid sometimes," Cole said.

"I don't care. That's not how we talk to each other," I went on. "And now you need to apologize to Casey."

"ALL RIGHT, ALL RIGHT, I'M SORRY!" he shouted, which wasn't exactly a model of penitent contrition.

At which point Casey began to cry in earnest.

When Cole saw that, his face softened, and he said simply, "I'm really sorry. I am."

So I let the two of them stew for a minute, and then I took the bookmark away. "You know why this is important, don't you?" I asked them before dumping the handy-dandy all-purpose guilt trip on them. "For one thing, it really pains me when you guys don't get along, because I know how much you really do love each other, deep down. And for another, there's going to be a time when Mommy and Daddy are not going to be here and all you're going to have is each other."

Silence for a long moment.

"You mean like when we go to camp?" Casey asked.

"No, like when we're *dead*," I replied.

I wasn't trying to scare her—I wanted to make sure she and Cole understood what I was trying to say. "My mother used to have the very same kind of talk with me and your aunt Tracy when we were little and getting in each other's hair. Your aunt Tracy and I used to fight like cats and dogs when we were younger, but now we're best friends. I love her and I can't imagine my life without her, but we went through a lot of tough times together."

"Like what?" Casey asked, even though I'd told them these stories many times.

Why is it that kids always want to hear about how naughty you were as a child? One trick to stop the bickering is to give juicy details of the time I, in a moment of blinding rage, knocked out one of Tracy's front teeth. (In my defense, it *was* loose at the time.) Or that charming occasion when we were out racing our bikes and she ran over the back of my leg when I fell off, then proceeded to win the race. This makes me small again, and it makes me their equal—someone they can relate to and process with more easily.

"Well," I said, settling back and putting my arms around them. "Even though Aunt Tracy used to drive me crazy, and I really got mad at my own mother for making me take her with me everywhere, I still always felt that I was in charge of taking care of her. And, deep down, that made me proud. I was *responsible* for her, you know? She often tells me about the time when I was in the fourth grade and she was in the third grade. I used to carry an umbrella in my red tote bag—there was a special spot for the umbrella in it.

"Anyway, I wasn't afraid to stand up to people, but Tracy was a lot shyer and soft-spoken and afraid to stick up for herself," I went on. "So she would often get hassled or bullied by some of the bigger kids at school. She tells me that if I saw that, I'd pull the umbrella out of my red tote bag and beat people up with it."

As they always did when I told them this story, Casey and Cole both burst out laughing.

"Did you do it a lot?" Cole asked.

"I don't remember doing it at all," I told him, "but if Aunt Tracy says that I did, it must have happened."

"Did she drive you crazy for a long time?"

"Not really," I said. "Our relationship got better as we got older. And then when our parents separated, Dad moved out and things changed, a lot. More than ever, Tracy and I had to care for each other. She really needed me. And that's when the tide changed.

"So that's when we remembered—and repeated—the words our mom had said to us. That one day she'd be gone, and all we'd have is each other.

"And you know what?" I added. "If you'd told me when I

was fourteen—when I really, really hated her guts!—that I'd miss Tracy terribly when we were grown-ups, I would have looked at you like you were completely crazy. But it's true. I wish that she didn't live in Fort Worth. It's too far for us to be able to see her more than twice a year, but I sure am glad whenever we get together."

I looked at Casey and Cole, then smiled. "I sure hope you two feel the same way about each other when you're grown-ups," I said sweetly.

Let's just say that there wasn't any more screaming, or name-calling, or hitting in the house.

For another forty-eight hours.

no sick days for mommy

I HOPE BY NOW THAT YOU'VE BEEN PRACTICING your "I Don't Care" mantra, because I'm about to drop another mantra on you. All moms can relate, because all moms have been there.

So, repeat after me: There Are No Sick Days for Mommy.

Now, the sooner you learn it and live it, the easier it'll be to manage your expectations about how everyone else is going to let you down during those terrible dark days when you can barely lift your fever-swimming head off the pillow.

I'll bet you didn't know that when you signed up to be a mother. You didn't realize There Are No Sick Days for Mommy. *Ever!* And if you live with a partner, the thing is, it's not just the kids you have to take care of.

The other night Buff was hacking and coughing. After putting up with this for several hours, I told him, "I think you're really sick."

"No, I'm not sick," he stubbornly insisted.

Despite the hacking, I managed to nod off. Until 1:04 a.m., when my dearest, darling husband woke me up from the precious little sleep I'd barely already gotten, leaned over me, and bemoaned in my face with germy breath, "I'm think I'm really sick."

Like, *duh!* I sure wouldn't have been so pissed off if he had listened to me earlier. He knew I had to be up and out the door in two-and-a-half hours, yet he was just now admitting he was sick, which meant that a certain chump (yours truly) needed to fling herself out of bed, find the aspirin and cough syrup and a glass of cool water, and proceed to shove them down his throat.

Along with the "There Are No Sick Days for Mommy" mantra comes this big, ugly, hairy news: Your children's world is predicated on the fact that nothing bad can or will happen to you. I think it's more critical for them that mothers stay healthy than it is for fathers. Why, I haven't figured out yet, but it's most likely because we're the primary caretakers, boo-boo soothers, and all-around servants to their every need. Their world would collapse if something terrible happened to us.

Every year, for instance, I'm first in line for my flu shot. There's no way I can up my risk for getting sick, not just because of my job but because of my caretaking at home. Buff's attitude to these shots, on the other hand, is that they're literally a pain and why bother—he knows *I'm* not going to get the flu!

Knowing I just can't get sick puts a tremendous burden of silent stress on me, as it's difficult to share these kinds of thoughts and fears with anyone but a select few trusted friends and loved ones. I remember what I used to worry about before I became a mom—my job, my friends, my figure, my love life. Once those little creatures arrive, however, there's a whole new meaning to the words "stress" and "worry." The stress can drive you straight to the chocolate bar, and the worry is like white noise. It never leaves you. And in the quiet, still moments when illness is creeping into your life, you can hear worry's terrifying sound thumping with every heartbeat—especially when your kids are sick. And you don't feel assuaged when your child suddenly develops a fever of 106 and the pediatrician you call in a panic sternly tells you to stop taking the child's temperature. Yeah, right, as if that's going to happen!

Cole has asthma that can flare from nonexistent to dire in about a nanosecond, and my television training—keeping my face and voice neutral while going out live, no matter whether I'm covering a natural disaster or the occasional crabby celebrity, even as producers and directors are barking directions into my earpiece and I have to wing it—has helped me be able to click into Calm Mommy mode, whether there's a scraped knee or a medical emergency. Luckily, both of my kids are pretty healthy, suffering from no more than the usual colds and other childhood crap that gets passed around.

This is particularly useful because my daughter is hypersensitive to anything remotely connected to pain. As a result, she's just about the world's worst patient. Once, she slid across the hardwood floor (while, naturally, I was squawking at her to cut it out), and inevitably a sliver ended up in the bottom of her foot.

Well, you'd think I was sawing off the leg of a soldier who'd just been wounded at Gettysburg, what with all the screaming and crying and carrying on. I had to literally turn that girl onto her stomach and smack her on the butt, as though she were the errant heroine of an old silent movie, to stop her from flailing around and doing more damage.

All because of a sliver of wood about an eighth of an inch long.

So, yeah, I do occasionally wonder, as moms do, how Casey might react if she's ever in a real accident. How hysterical will she become? Will I manage to instantly click into Calm Mommy mode to comfort her?

I think the maternal instinct kicks in the minute there's any kind of pain—the instinct to kiss it away and make it all better. But when accidents or illnesses rear their ugly heads, you often feel powerless to help. Often, you *are* powerless. You'd willingly trade places with your child in a flash if you could, but you can't.

Living with this feeling can be tough for a good-enough mother, who fervently believes that whatever she's doing is good enough. Sickness flips that philosophy on its head. Whatever you're doing might *not* be good enough (unless you're a pediatrician, a surgeon, or another health-care practitioner), and as a result, your vulnerabilities and fears can be overwhelming.

I know this firsthand. When Cole gets any plain old respiratory virus, it can become lethal. He was diagnosed with asthma when he was a baby, but it never gave him any trouble until we first moved to the New York area, and Hurricane Isabel parked itself right overhead, dropping tropical moisture along with just about everything it had churned up. (I didn't know it then, but Cole's pulmonologist later told me that the intense drop in barometric pressure during hurricanes can trigger asthma attacks.) Cole went from bad to worse in less than twenty minutes, and after I raced him to the emergency room, he was admitted to the ward where six other asthmatic children lay gasping for breath. I could barely relax, even when I saw that Cole's situation wasn't as dire as some of the other kids', who were trying to get comfortable under oxygen tents. I still have never been so scared in my entire life as I was when I sat gently stroking Cole's head while he threw up all over me and the puke bucket for three nights straight.

Fortunately, Cole quickly recovered, and now he talks proudly about his stint in the hospital. It took me a lot longer to recuperate. The whole thing was such a terrible learning experience, with me feeling totally inadequate as a mother, wasting endless hours kicking myself for not knowing any better. Where had I been during the Asthma 101 Emergency Course? Thankfully, Cole has never had another asthma attack, and now that I can recognize the symptoms, I have a protocol in place to start treating them right away if they arise.

Even though Cole has had many more illnesses due to this asthma, he's a much better, more stoic patient than his sister. As long as he gets extra candy and a little bit of extra attention, he's fine.

This is what I told myself when Cole got sent home from camp last summer after he suddenly developed a high fever. By the time I got home, Cole was swaddled under blankets and looking as if he'd been run over by a parade, poor boy. He was too miserable to even want to watch *SpongeBob*. Immediately I felt the panic rise, and just as quickly, I damped it down so he wouldn't be able to tell how scared I was to see my little boy—who's usually being told to get his butt down from whatever piece of furniture he's climbed up—lying prone and wan in bed.

Cole is resilient, thank goodness, and he was soon up and around and breaking things with his usual spontaneity.

But it's not always so easy for moms to get right back to normal. Taking care of sick kids is always the working mother's nightmare—not only the worry about their condition when we're stuck in the office but also the worry about the logistics of finding someone to take care of them when we're stuck in the office. I'm extremely lucky and thankful I have Consuelo, a full-time employee who lives nearby and has a car, so she can swing by to pick up the kids and watch them as needed until Buff or I can get home.

Lots of other working moms, however, do not have a full-time child-care worker. When their kids are sick, it can be a life-threatening issue, not just for the child with the flu but also for those who simply cannot afford to lose their jobs by taking necessary time off. Working moms often end up taking their own sick days or risking getting fired so they can care for their ill kids.

Proof, of course, that There Are No Sick Days for Mommy.

My suggestion is that all working moms have not just one but several backup plans in place. I've learned this from unfortunate experience—when Consuelo has been sick herself, Buff's been away, and I wasn't able to leave the studio. Somehow, my children still had to be picked up from school and watched until I could arrive home.

The backup for my backup is pretty simple—I have several friends on speed-dial whose kids are the same ages as my kids. I know I can count on them in emergencies, and vice versa. Although I of course prefer to be able to manage my family on my own, if there's a problem—like someone, a parent or a child, becoming ill—then I'm not too proud to ask for assistance. I admit that I'm in a bind, and ask if they'd mind helping out. No one has ever said no. We all know what it's like.

Because There Are No Sick Days for Mommy!

I see my backup friends as a sort of Venn diagram of safety nets—they all overlap. If I suddenly get sick, or one of the kids gets sick, the calls go out. First to Consuelo, then to Buff, then to Friend A, Friend B, Friend C. Someone on the list will be able to make sure my kids are safe. If I'm sick, I'll be able to get the rest I need, and if the kids are sick, they'll be able to be tucked into bed, spreading their germs in someone else's house until I can arrive to fumigate the sickroom.

Fortunately, no one's ever come down with the flu after my kids have coughed all over them, and my friends and I have shared some rueful conversations, long after the adrenaline has mercifully worn off, about late-night runs to the emergency room. We all agree that for any mom there's no scare worse than taking your child to the emergency room, especially if you have a child with a chronic disease. Kids can get sick so fast with a wheeze or a suspicious rash or a superhigh fever, or they fall and break a bone, or they get food poisoning and dehydrated, and even when you had nothing to do with whatever happened, it's still hard not to blame yourself for not being a perfect, omniscient mother who could somehow have woven a magic bubble of protectiveness over her precious brood 24/7. Being able to commiserate with your friends about your fears is probably the best way to dispel them.

Some emergency room visits are good for laughs—in retrospect. We had a neighbor with a daredevil daughter, one whose name was practically emblazoned on the walls of the local ER because she'd been there so many times in need of another splint or a cast or stitches. Her poor mom still hasn't recuperated from the mortification after the time her dearest daredevil daughter stuck a raisin up her nose. Turns out that raisins up the nose can be dangerous (who knew?), because if they get stuck in the sinuses, they can trigger a massive infection, and surgery becomes the only way to get them out.

"So, which nostril?" the attending doctor asked.

The mom was so freaked out and frazzled that she couldn't remember which one. Nor could her dearest daredevil daughter, who thought the whole thing was terribly funny.

I can top that, because one of my kids is allergic to penicillin. Okay, it's Cole. After being his mom for nearly nine years, you'd think I'd know that by now, but when I took him to the emergency room the last time I thought he was having an asthma attack, I completely blanked. The nurses in triage were asking me if Cole had any allergies, and I was busy having a total senior moment, brought on by the stress of the situation, in the middle of the emergency room.

"Okay, okay," I finally said. "I have two children and *one* of them is allergic to penicillin."

"Are you sure you have two children?" the nurse asked sarcastically.

Sheesh. She could have cut me some slack since I stood there like a panicking wild woman. Which is also what I turned into when Cole got sent home sick from camp. Turned out he just had some virus that was going around. I told Buff that he needed to pick up some children's Tylenol on his way home and give it to Cole. Exhausted from the stress of the day, I fell asleep. In the morning I checked on Cole, whose fever had mercifully broken, and I asked Buff when he'd given Cole the dose so I'd know when he was due for the next one.

"Oh, I couldn't find the Tylenol, so I gave him aspirin," Buff casually informed me.

"WHAT!" I screamed. "Are you out of your mind? Children are *never* supposed to take aspirin—they can get Reye's syndrome and brain damage. The only people who should ever take children's aspirin are you and me. What is *wrong* with you?"

"You told me to give him aspirin," Buff said with a pout.

I heaved a sigh and stomped off to bed. The only person right then who really needed an aspirin was yours truly.

but can she juggle? hell, yes!

IT'S RAINING OUTSIDE. I'M TRAVELING ON assignment this upcoming weekend. I get to work, rush into hair and makeup so I will look marginally awake, pull on my pants. *Rip!* Just what I needed—a hole! *Crap.* It's 6:43 a.m., and I have to be upstairs and camera-ready by 6:50 a.m. Seven minutes and counting. I whip off the pants and hand them to my most trusted lieutenant, in the form of my assistant, Jahayra, who races down to wardrobe to get the britches stitched.

As I sit in my undergarments, going through scripts for the show, the phone rings. It's Consuelo, my other trusted lieutenant, in the form of the kids' babysitter. She's crying so hard I can't even understand her. Finally I get her to calm down, and she tells me that she's been at the hospital all night due to severe, debilitating pain from several cysts and is on her way to the house but doesn't think she's up to working. *Crap.* I tell her to go home, then jab Buff's number faster than I thought humanly possible, and tell him that Consuelo is in extreme pain and can't get there, so can he please stay until the kids get on the school bus (oh, by the way, it's now 6:46 a.m. and I still have no pants)?

Working in live television, I've had many, many moments over the years when I'm screaming on the inside, yet you'd look at me and think, *Hey, that lady's got her act together.* Ha! But I've learned to wing it. No one who goes live in front of a television camera ever has total control over how any situation will unfold, but we get up there and face the cameras anyway. Flying-by-the-seat-of-your-pants TV has been excellent training for crisis management and spontaneous reactions. I've always had to remain calm and collected, even when dealing with the inner screaming, and have had to put on my public face and refrain from saying "crap" aloud when something or everything goes wrong.

That's the way the news business is—and we just do it.

Kind of an apt metaphor for good-enough mothering, don't you think? After all, good-enough mothers trust their instincts. They can manage spur-of-the-moment catastrophes and spills. They're like octopi, with one arm reaching for the phone, one reaching for the keyboard to send another e-mail, one reaching for the paperwork, one reaching for a crying child. Although they rarely give themselves enough credit for it, good-enough mothers become so adept at multitasking that they're no longer even aware of how many balls they're juggling at the same time with finesse and grace.

Even when work is incredibly stressful, I wouldn't have it any other way. I *have* to work. It's who I am. I love working in television and I love the excitement of going out live and reaching people, and I've even grown to love winging it. No way will I consider giving up my career to be a full-time stay-at-home mother. I totally understand any mom who wants to do that, but it isn't me.

Earning a living isn't just about feeding my family; it's about feeding my heart, brain, and soul.

But—and this is a big "but"—no matter how much I love my work, it will always be my second-most important job. My job encapsulates what every working good-enough mother lives with on a daily basis: professional satisfaction for me, coupled with worries of not being there for my husband and children. I know that once any woman becomes a mom, *that's* always going to be job numero uno. You're still responsible for making sure the trains run on time at home, the kids have clean underwear, there's food in the fridge that may even have some vitamin content, and the homework gets done before the TV goes on.

The trick (and boy is it tricky!) is finding a healthy balance between the demands of the job you love and the kids you love more.

I never thought of not working—it wasn't part of the work ethic drilled into my sister and me. Nor do I think about retiring—it's inconceivable to think about days that aren't spent doing something productive, not just for me but for others.

Much of this pragmatic work ethic comes from my mom, the original good-enough mother. She liked going to work. (She still volunteers on a regular basis.) She liked her weekends off too. Even though she and my dad had a fractious relationship, they both gave me unconditional love and support and the belief that I could succeed, if I worked hard and kept at it.

I didn't know I was going to be a journalist. After getting my BA in psychology from California State University, Sacramento, in 1987, I thought working as a therapist might be a viable career. While working the night shift for a local suicide hotline, it suddenly dawned on me that I didn't want to be a therapist—I wanted to parlay my skills (writing talent, an outgoing and naturally curious nature, good listening technique) into something else. I preferred to think that didn't mean I was a snoop with a big mouth, but that, maybe, those were the kinds of skills that could turn me into a good reporter.

The very next morning I switched from psychology to communications, talked myself into a nonpaying intern job at a local independent station, where the kindly souls there taught me TV 101 in about six months, then landed my first job. Years later, I was offered work in Dallas, first at the ABC affiliate (for four years) and then at the CBS affiliate, where I ended up as the noon and six p.m. anchor for nearly five years.

Although my ABC contract hadn't been renewed and I was technically unemployed when I became pregnant with Casey, I never considered not getting another job and going back on the air. I spent her first five months with her, and by that point I was really ready to get back to work. With Cole, I had only ten weeks off, and because Cole was practically glued to my nipples for all of that time, I was really, *really* ready to get back to work.

Part of the reason was that I had a great nanny. I really lucked out when I was pregnant with Casey. I worked out while pregnant with both kids right up until the week before each of them popped out, and the nanny at the gym's nursery where I worked out while I was pregnant with Casey was looking for a new job. Jeannie stayed with us for five years, and we all loved her like the fifth member of our family. Consuelo has since taken over.

Now, no working mother can possibly cope with the stress of working (no matter how much you love it) without sorting out the child-care situation. Having adequate child-care can enable you to move seamlessly from home to job, while not having it can become an absolute nightmare, where your paycheck can be jeopardized because you're chronically late to work because of scheduling conflicts between your kids' school and your inflexible boss.

Just think about the demands your kids' schools make. First of all, the school day ends in the midafternoon. Does your job? I doubt it. Then there are parent-teacher conferences, birthday parties, class field trips, open houses, school plays, book fairs, early dismissal days, and constant days off for national holidays and school breaks. And, of course, you want to be at the school as much as you can be, because it's important for your children and because you need to keep your finger on the pulse of the school dynamic and your children's interactions with teachers and classmates.

So who's going to watch the kids when they need watching?

Rare indeed is the employer who'll be lenient when it comes to employees who need regular time off to attend school events. Plus, you already know that There Are No Sick Days for Mommy. Things can go wrong for anyone. Babysitters and kids get sick or have accidents. Cars break down or traffic gets backed up when there's an accident or subways stall. Lots of moms don't have the options that I do, and when their kids are sick or need extra attention, something's got to give— usually Mom's sanity. As a result, even the most satisfying job can become a never-ending source of stress if worries about proper child care consume your days.

It's taken me years to establish a pretty much infallible system of backup for the child care, and to not be too inhibited to speak up when I've needed help the most. I've been fortunate to find loving and reliable nannies, and friends I can call on in emergencies. Other moms find great day care situations where their kids thrive in a social setting before going off to a more structured school. Others rely on reliable after-school babysitters, after-school activities, relatives, or friends who have more flexible schedules to oversee the child care.

I think more than anything, a good-enough mother learns to trust her gut when it comes to who watches the kids. Some moms insist on using pricey agencies to find nannies, and they ignore the little nagging voices that tell them that the nanny might not be a great fit even though she costs a fortune. Sometimes child-care workers are great on paper, with impeccable references, but they just don't get along with your kids, or vice versa. Or they might rub you the wrong way. Or the staff at the day care center has a high turnover.

I trusted my gut with Jeannie, and had no trouble leaving the house to go to work. And so, one bright day in 2002, I was driving to the studio after having spent a hellacious morning at the dentist, when Henry, my agent, called with the stunning news that CBS in New York was interested in talking to me about an opening at *The Early Show*. Turns out that he was being a good agent—after reading an article about CBS revamping their morning show, he'd sent off my reel.

Was I thrilled and surprised? You bet. So what did I say?

"But, Henry, we just built a house!"

Buff and I had spent the last year building our too-big house, and had spent countless hours overseeing it, from conception to the final coats of paint. We'd moved in a scant four months before.

"René!" he said, justifiably scolding me. "Just go up there and talk to them!"

Off I went for my interview. Much to my delight, I was soon offered the job that would transform my career.

Still, there was a huge logistical problem. Buff had a great job in Dallas. Our kids loved living there. We had built ourselves a home—not just the house but as part of a vibrant community.

But just because I have children and a husband doesn't mean my dreams die when theirs are born. Buff and I had hours and hours of spirited discussions, trying to figure out what to do. And then we put together a plan that involved my accepting the job and devoting the necessary energy to it, yet still being a viable presence in my kids' life.

I've always felt that failure and disappointment, as well as leaps of faith and well-thought-out risk-taking, are powerful teaching tools. I look back on my life and I think that the times when I did the most growing as a person and a professional were the times I was at a major crossroads. This happened to be one of those crossroads. I had to confront whatever it was that needed changing and improvement.

And I also know that the best progress I've made in my life, and the most satisfaction, has come from the choices I made that were risky. If I didn't try, then how could I learn?

So I made the choice that was right for me, risky as it might have been, and I commuted. With Buff's encouragement and blessing. For eight months.

No way was I going to lose out on such a fantastic work

opportunity, so Buff and I made the decision that the kids would finish out the school year, and we'd put the house on the market while I scouted around for another one. We also wanted to give his company time to make or find him a job.

Yet when I told my friends and colleagues that this was the plan, I hate to report that the near-universal reaction wasn't "What a marvelous job you'll have!" but "How are you going to leave your kids for so long?"

Taken aback, I questioned why when men did this kind of thing (all the time), they were rarely (if ever) questioned about the effect *their* absences might have on their families. I'd be seeing Casey and Cole every weekend. It wasn't a permanent situation. My children would be well looked-after. Their dad was still going to be with them. It would be for only eight months.

Well, the silence was deafening. The double standard appalled and infuriated me, actually. I became more determined than ever to succeed at my new job, not just because it was something I wanted so badly, but to prove the hypocritical skeptics wrong!

I knew that taking the job at *The Early Show* was the best thing that had happened to me professionally, but I've got to be perfectly honest and admit that commuting was hell. It was hell for the kids and my husband, who missed me like crazy. It was hard for me, who missed them like crazy. Not just emotionally but physically. The commute was taxing, to put it mildly. By Thursday night I'd be aflush with adrenaline, excited because on Friday afternoon I'd be on my way home. I'd sleep all the way to Dallas, and then I would try to be awake for the kids on Friday night, when we'd do something as a family. Saturday was great, but that night I'd start to get that anxious feeling in the pit of my stomach that meant I had to get ready to go.

Now that I no longer need to commute, I'd say that the hardest thing about balancing work and family is still the fatigue factor. Sometimes I wonder how I'm going to summon the energy to be upbeat on the air in the morning, and not lose my patience when I have to do the shopping and the cooking and the pickups from playdates and the trips to the orthodontist and the chasing of the dog who's just stolen another shoe and the preparation for the next morning's schedule. The only way to manage the hectic demands of daily life is to eat smart, keep my body healthy with regular workouts, get enough sleep, and make sure I have some downtime alone. (So, okay, I spend most of the downtime deep in slumber, but I made this bed and I'm sure as heck gonna lie in it!)

Since Casey and Cole have had a working mother from day one, they're used to the fact that I work. They know I love my work too, even when it's demanding, which is a big plus when it comes to getting them to finish homework they find frustrating or annoying. That's just how it is in our family. And actually, because of my odd schedule, I'm able to spend a lot of time with them. Plus I don't have to work weekends, except when I'm on the road.

Sticking to a routine helps, especially for the kids when I'm off on assignment. When Casey and Cole were little, I didn't travel as much, but now I'm probably gone once a month, or sometimes working late nights. I can explain why I have to go, and where, and they get it. Thank goodness for cell phones, which make communication so much easier. To say nothing of my beloved, well-thumbed BlackBerry. (Without my phone and BlackBerry, I feel as though I'm on the dark side of the moon.) I give my kids, Buff, and Consuelo my schedule, and make sure they always know where I am at any given moment, as well as how to reach me. Getting an e-mail from Casey can brighten up even the dreariest trek through an airport. And the time she e-mailed me to tell me she was proud of me left me practically bawling at security!

On the other hand, as I've said before and will say again, my kids need time away from me just as much as I need it from them. You know, that whole absence-makes-the-heart-grow-fonder thing is really true. In order for children to become fully actualized human beings, they need to learn apart from their parents. They can be given all the love, care, and nurturing that parents can bestow to the best of their abilities, but they've got to learn to stand on their own two feet, find their own path to happiness, and discover what it is they're good at and want to become in life.

I hope that by seeing me as a working mom who derives tremendous satisfaction from her work, even when her pants are ripped, my children will be better able to have confidence in their own skills as they grow older.

Having time apart is as important as preserving your own sense of space while at home. Casey and Cole love me, but sometimes that physical love can be smothering. The other night we were all doing something, and they were stacked on top of me. After a while, I couldn't take it any longer and kicked them out.

"Please, I need some space," I told them. "Go find your father. He just got home."

Is this blasphemous? Heck, no. It's the truth.

Well, okay, I would have preferred a little smothering during a recent jaunt. See, while busting my tail to get to Billings, Montana, for a shoot, I called home. After spending about five seconds dispensing with niceties (as in, "What did you get us?"), Casey and Cole both informed me they *had* to have playdates the next day, which meant the playdates had to be organized by me, sometime in the twenty minutes it was going to take me to traverse the Denver airport to catch my connecting flight, while wearing a heavy coat and schlepping two heavy bags, cell phone glued to my ear. Then I had to call Cole back while navigating the long line of a public restroom so I could listen to him tell me about the research he had done on Africa. Yep, my kids have my time and attention, even in an airport bathroom.

An image of one of those cartoon octopi flashed in my head—yeah, that's what I needed. Four arms could run like the wind to get to the gate while the others could work the phone and BlackBerry.

Crap, I thought. *What are the phone numbers of their friends so I can set up those playdates? Why, oh why, didn't I plug them into my BlackBerry when I could have? That would have been too easy!*

So there I was, frantically trying to remember the phone numbers while jumping aboard an available cart to get to the gate on time. I finally got the numbers right, called the parents, made the dates, arranged the transportation, called the kids, got them up to speed on the plans, listened to them haggling about who got to talk to me a nanosecond longer, ran onto the plane, finally took a deep breath, downed a glass of wine, and promptly fell asleep before I could congratulate myself on being a little bit better than good enough.

Still, as much as I want to be by myself on my travels, when I come back, I'm ready to come back. I am fully recharged as soon as I see the beaming faces of my little cherubs and give them a kiss and a long, long hug. It takes at least half an hour of pure bliss before the "COLE PARHAM, YOU GET HERE RIGHT THIS MINUTE!" somehow manages to escape from my mouth.

Welcome home, Mom!

home is where the heart is

MY DECORATING STYLE IS WHAT I LIKE TO CALL "casually elegant."

If you can read between the lines, what that means is that nothing in my house matches. Not the cloth napkins, not the cups, not the cutlery.

At the Parham estate, among the things that we always give thanks for on Thanksgiving is that we found six unbroken plates and that no one gets food poisoning.

Anyone who stays with me will soon realize that in terms of creature comforts, they're gonna get more frills at a Girl Scouts' campground than at my house. Most of them are okay with this.

For instance, my mother, Anne Syler, knows that if she wants fitted and top sheets that match, she'd better bring them from home. My stepdaughter, Tracy, knows she'll be sleeping on a futon that my son Cole has christened on more than one occasion over the years. And the towels in the guest bathroom will be nice and soft and frayed around the edges, because I bought them during the first Bush Administration.

Fancy-schmancy "could be on the cover of *Architectural*

Digest" decorating is not my forte, nor will it ever be. Most of our furniture arrived straight from the fumigator after being dug up at a flea market, or from Costco. I sometimes glance through shelter magazines, marveling at the all-white sofas, or the impractical stain-daring carpeting, and quickly turn the pages, secure in the knowledge that whoever came up with beige never had children who love grape juice.

When it comes to our home, I am all about function over form. Plus, how I see my house is a reflection of how I see my family.

When Buff and I got married, we made a pact that wherever we lived, our house would be our castle, and we'd build a (metaphorical) moat around it. At the end of the day, we could retreat and feel safe. Our home is comfy and lived-in and filled with love. No room is off-limits to anyone, even a shoe-chomping nutcase of a dog, and there's nothing in our home that can't be jumped on, laid on with bare (filthy-from-outdoors) feet, or covered in dog hair. The Parham estate is a place where one can be healed and recharged. It's a place where we can sprawl around and be comfortable and feel good about being there while talking to one another. It's also a place where we can all snipe at one another even while knowing that it's okay and that everyone still loves everyone else.

When we lived in Dallas, I poured my heart and soul into helping design a wonderful house that was a whopping fifty-five-hundred square feet in size. We thought it would be fun to have so much space, but we were wrong. The house was incredible, but it was just too big for four, and as a result, it felt more like a showcase than a *home*. The kids felt lost in it. We ended up spending all our time in the kitchen, which actually wasn't the most comfortable room, to combat the isolating feeling of empty sprawl. I also realized that when you live in a too-big house, where the master suite is on one floor and the kids' rooms are on another floor, and they each have their own bathrooms, you don't have to worry about getting in one another's faces. Sounds good in theory, especially when you finally have the vast closets of your dreams, but when you practically have to take a bus to find your kids, it's no way to solve any conflicts.

Plus, it makes you feel lonely in your own home.

So when I got the job at CBS in New York, I knew what I wanted. A homey house. One where I could put the family back in the family room, the heart and soul of the house. See, an excruciatingly important point I'd learned from our too-big house was that we basically only need one room. Whatever room I'm in, the kids will eventually follow me, pied-piper-like. I swear, they have a specific radar that dings whenever I crawl into my work chair after dinner and try to settle down to get something done. There the three of us will sit, crammed into my office, the teeniest room in the house. And we're perfectly contented. Sometimes Buff will join in, so that brings the body count up to four.

I guess it's true that home is where the heart is.

So I spent many long weekends on the Metro-North commuter trains, scouting around for the right place for us to live. I wanted my kids to grow up in a house with a yard, as I had, in an area with good schools, yet the house had to be easily accessible to the cultural diversity of a large metropolis. And when I finally found The House, it just felt right. Our home in the suburb that I call Picketfenceville is old and lovely. Not anywhere as huge as our Dallas house, but comfortable.

Our one room has turned out to be the kitchen. I learned my lesson. We put a large, comfy, ugly, and (most important) easy-to-clean sofa in there, which is usually covered with dog hair and the detritus dumped out from the bottom of the kids' backpacks, but it's still an inviting room. There's a lovely view out the windows to the patio and the trees in the backyard. It's the kind of room that invites relaxation (and the inhalation of too many sweets stolen from the cupboard).

And in our home, mess is where the heart is too. Okay, so sue me. I've always been that way. From the time I popped out of the womb, I was a messy kid. I had a messy crib, a messy playpen, a messy child's room, and now I have a messy house. That's just me.

Unlike some of my friends, who get some perverse satisfaction from *daily* dusting (I'm *not* going there!), I usually derive no pleasure from housekeeping. Thank goodness Buff likes to do the laundry. He'll fold everything impeccably, and then put it away in perfectly aligned stacks. Folding? Forget about it.

Once every blue moon or so I'll get this weird hankering to iron. First it'll take about an hour to find the iron. Then another hour to find the ironing board, which is about as rusty as Cole's bike after he left it out in the rain one weekend too many. Then I'll stand there like a robot and iron all the kids' clothes and my clothes with a spray-starched vengeance.

That won't happen again for about another two years.

But then again, sometimes when I'm ironing, or when I find myself with a dust rag in hand, I understand the need to clean—and not just to get rid of the cobwebs. It can be deeply satisfying to lose yourself in a mindless activity. It's sort of like meditation in motion. There is, after all, so much of the *intangible* to raising children, hoping that they'll make it to adulthood as wise and wonderful people who managed to get through the teenage years without crashing the car or becoming addicted to cigarettes and instant messaging. I can't predict what lessons of today are going to make a dent in tomorrow. But I can predict the simple pleasure of setting simple goals and reaching them.

Especially eradicating all the dust bunnies under the beds, a noteworthy event that happens, oh, about once every two years when I bother to find the broom.

Poor Buff has given up on seeing me with a broom in hand. Worse (for him), he's a neat freak. He has to put up with my mess. He's practically been a saint for all these years, because I try to make an effort, but I still end up dressing off the floor. Sometimes I'm careful to give him the heads-up prior to his re-entry after being away for a long weekend. "Please don't start bitching the minute you get in the door," I'll tell him over the phone. "I just want you to know that the house is a disaster." Okay, I'll spare him the details about our jaunts to the toy store, which mean the living room is overflowing with Styrofoam, and Cole has already broken or lost half the pieces of his LEGO set.

Buff still can't figure out how I do it, but I always know where everything is in the piles. Once the piles reach a certain critical mass of mess, however—usually when I can't find my prescription medications and my vitamins and my favorite black bra—then even I can't take it anymore, and I spend a crabby, grumbling afternoon doing a massive cleanup.

The cleanliness will last for about a week or so, and then the mess starts growing again.

My dearest husband spends an inordinate amount of time teaching our kids that mess is not to be tolerated. It is one task I am happy to abdicate, since they do need to learn how to pick up after themselves, and God knows they are not going to find the best example in me! (I realize this might sound a little bit hypocritical, since I am Ms. Messy. But even though there are times when you know you aren't exactly setting a good example, that doesn't mean you should be cutting your kids any slack because of your own bad habits. I know that if Buff weren't the Mess-master, I'd have to get my act together and really clean it up.)

So we have rules: If the kids want their allowances, they have to put their dirty clothes away in the hamper, and they have to manage to keep all their stuff kind of together. Even when they were toddlers, hypocrite that I am, I'd say to my kids, "That goes back in the toy box." If they can take it out, then they can figure out how to put it back!

See, I don't mind if they tear up their rooms as long as they straighten up the mess later. Just so they don't think they can tear it up and leave it. Or expect me to tidy up after them. Well, actually, they know *that* isn't going to happen!

Luckily, Casey is just like Buff when it comes to tidiness, and her room is as neat as a pin. I don't have to ask her twice where her shoes are.

But let's not go into Cole's room right now.

Still, it's hard to complain about anyone else's mess when I can't often manage my own. Because I don't have an overwhelming desire to clean up after whatever or whoever makes the mess in the first place (you know, clutter and the stuff that just sort of piles up for no reason), I have a hard time with what becomes the *redundancy* of more mess constantly reappearing. (And, it goes without saying, I have no one to blame but myself.)

What drives me bonkers in our house, besides the lack of closet space, is the redundancy of the ketchup bottles, the jars of relish, and the piles of cheese. When I'm in the supermarket, I can never remember if I already have something, so I figure I might as well buy it, and then we'll end up with four dozen of the same thing. People think I have some sort of sickness. The other day I looked into the refrigerator and saw four ketchup bottles. Three of them were full. And then I looked in another cupboard, and Consuelo (a neat freak like Buff, thank goodness!) had lined up all the soaps. There were seven squirt bottles of liquid soap. Who needs seven bottles of liquid soap? Yet we'll run out of detergent.

And, of course, we'll have three bottles of children's Tylenol, and then as soon as one of the kids gets sick, I'll open a jar only to find it empty.

Just like the other two.

breaking the (piggy) bank

MY DAD WAS A FISCALLY RESPONSIBLE KIND OF guy. He'd always say, "You can't buy that, you can't spend money on that." It drove my mom bonkers. Not that she was extravagant, but she hated having to pinch pennies. One time she had to go to bat over a swing set. Back when I was growing up, we lived in Sacramento, in a safe neighborhood where no one locked their doors in the afternoon and kids spent the after-school hours running in and out of everyone else's homes to play. We had a big backyard and neighbors who all had swing sets. Dad said forget about it. Mom said we needed to swing.

We got the swing set, and I got a good lesson in how to negotiate.

Both parents instilled a work ethic in me that exists to this day—one that I hope I pass on to my own children. My parents believed that you have a duty in life to work hard, and that nobody owes you anything, and that you do the work you get. If I wanted money, I was going to have to earn it myself.

Even though I knew this was sound, moral advice, it wasn't always easy to live with as a child and teenager, not when half the kids I knew were given cars for their sweet sixteens or when they went off to college. My parents couldn't afford to buy me a car, so I had to buy my own with money earned at crummy fast-food restaurant jobs. I did it even if all I could afford was a beat-up old hunk of junk. But I am not sorry I worked my way up.

I will, however, be very sorry if my children don't grow up to viscerally understand how vitally important this ethic is, and to know what real hard work is, and how you have to get up and go do it even when you aren't in the mood.

I don't think that a lot of Casey and Cole's peers understand the difference between "want" and "need." They haven't lived hand-to-mouth as I once did. They don't *need* another pair of shoes unless the pair they're wearing gets holes and tears, but they think they do, because they *want* the Heelys or Crocs or whatever kind of shoe everyone else seems to be parading around in. I know it's part of my job and my responsibility as a good-enough mother to get this point drilled into my kids' sweet little Heelys-demanding heads.

So when Casey and Cole asked me if we were rich, I knew what to say.

"You are rich, because you have a family who loves you," I told them. "Why, what do you think?"

"I think we're rich because we have a big house," Cole offered.

"Well, you know that may be so, but that's not what true wealth is about, is it?"

And then, as their eyes grew larger, I went into my spiel about how it's my job to bring them up and make them well-adjusted human beings. And I told them that I'd love to say that it was also my job to make them happy, but only they are responsible for their own happiness. And I want them to be able to handle whatever life throws at them and to really understand that life is a gift and how fortunate they are. They have the opportunity to get a great education; they have a family with two parents who love them, and an extended family who loves them too.

The money aspect of what makes them rich is way, way down at the bottom of the list. Money, I explained, is to be respected but not idolized.

And the kind of satisfaction and deep happiness you get in life is all the more sweet when it's been earned. If it has been earned, it has a richness that is more wonderful than all the gold in Fort Knox.

Try explaining that lofty concept to an eight-year-old who has drawn up his Christmas wish list in May.

Of course when I talk to my kids about money, I don't quite go into the details of how I used to (mis)manage my own financial affairs prior to my marriage. For someone who was in her thirties at the time, I really should have been much more together. I made good money, but I never knew where any of it went. I swear, I'd get bills but I wouldn't open them. Instead, I'd dump them into a shoe box, and every few months I'd force myself to sit down and take care of it, not thinking about what I was paying in late fees and how I was stupidly trashing my credit rating. How dumb was that? It was really an idiotic way to behave, the full ramifications of which didn't hit home until we were trying to buy one, and we nearly couldn't get a mortgage. Only Buff's stellar record saved the day.

I'm determined that Casey and Cole will not have such a haphazard attitude toward money. I believe a small allowance is a useful tool, because kids need to understand that moms and/or dads earn money. They also need to understand the true value of what things cost, and that money may be crucial for life's necessities, but that a lot of people will have different ideas about what things are essential.

And no, designer skateboards and designer denim are *not* essential.

Unlike our parents, our kids are growing up with the convenience of ATMs. I walk up to a machine and punch in some numbers and out pops money. But I've taught them that the bank isn't just being nice to me because I'm such a fabulous person. That's *my* money—I've earned every penny of it.

So Casey and Cole have to do their chores if they want their allowances. That's the deal. Their chores are pretty easy, things like setting and clearing the dinner table. Or making sure their rooms aren't total disaster areas. Or feeding the dog. I had to take the trash out when I was a kid, and I hated it with such a passion—no plastic garbage bags back then in the Middle Ages, so it stank and leaked—that I've spared them that particular misery, even though our bags don't leak. Still, as they grow older, I'll add more complicated tasks.

Bottom line: Children *need* chores. They need to know they're an important cog in the wheel that makes the house hum.

Olivia has reaped the rewards for Cole's lackadaisical attitude toward her mealtime. A while back I asked him to feed the dog, and he grumbled and didn't do it the right way, so he had to be hauled back to do it a second time.

"Lazy people work twice as hard," I told him.

"What do you mean?" he asked, puzzled.

"I mean that instead of doing it right the first time, you had to come back and feed her again. You had to do the exact same thing twice because you were too lazy to care about getting it right the first time. See?"

He nodded. He got it.

I hope he'll remember that lesson when he's a teenager and I kick him out the door to get a job. He's not going to be a slacker when he can be out there earning his keep! For me, it won't even be a question of letting Cole and Casey get jobs. They'll *have* to work if they want to buy any of the non-essential junk such as little flashing lights for their cell phones or an iPod the size of a fingernail or whatever else will become ultratrendy by the time Casey and Cole hit those formative years.

My kids learned how serious I was about respecting money when they couldn't find their own. Casey used an old can as a piggy bank, and Cole kept his money in a little box. Somehow the can and the box kept getting knocked off the shelves when the kids were playing or horsing around, and the coins would end up all over the place, where they would remain for days if I didn't get on Casey and Cole to pick them up and put them away. Fed up, I swooped in one day, counted up their loose change, and informed them that from then on, since they had demonstrated a sincere lack of interest in their funds, their money was going to be kept safe, in the bank. I took them to the local bank and showed them how to open an account. Now I let them accumulate their allowance and then dump it in there when it's convenient. It was an excellent lesson in responsibility.

Here's where I actually run into trouble. I can't figure out which things I should let them buy with their own money and which things I should buy. Part of that is my working-mom's guilt. I want to do and get nice things for my kids because I do feel guilty every now and then for not being there and spending enough time with them. So I have been known to overcompensate.

On the other hand, it's easier to draw the line when you hear the little darlings spouting the pitch for the latest toy or gizmo they've seen on the endless commercials on television. That our consumer culture of consumption can seep so easily into their pores and consciousnesses is a real dilemma. I mean, sometimes the kids will be watching a great educational show about wildlife or science and the commercials still scream, "BUY ME! BUY ME NOW!"

So when the kids ask me to "BUY IT NOW!" I swiftly tell them that money has a place, and its place is in the bank, and if they want something superspecial, they can save up the money to buy it themselves or put it on their birthday/holiday wish list. At some point, you just have to put the brakes on.

And it's also hard for me to not step in to show them what I think is the best use of their money. Example: I owed Casey a toy (payment for her being so well-behaved during the photo shoot for this book), and she said she wanted a Game Boy. Well, I had to bite my tongue to stop from blurting out that she already had not one but two different versions and why on earth would she want another. Then she told me herself.

"It's pink," she said.

Oh, don't be so ridiculous, I thought. *Who cares if it's pink on the outside if the inside is the same?* And then I realized, hold on, it's her decision to make. She earned it—she can do what she wants with it. If she bought the Game Boy, she'd quickly weary of the pink cover once she realized that it didn't do anything new, but it would be too late to exchange it. But she would have learned a valuable lesson about what true value is, and that impulsive actions have unforeseen consequences, and how appearances can be deceiving.

I'm glad I kept quiet, because she decided to buy a game cartridge instead and to save the rest of the money for a PSP that I'll no doubt be clueless as to how to operate.

Hopefully her attitude will rub off on Cole. It's harder for him to focus on saving, as he's much more impulsive.

On the other hand, he'll probably do just fine. When my stepdaughter, Tracy, asked Cole to be in her wedding, he thought about it for a minute.

"You want me to carry that silly pillow with the ring on it?" he asked her, and she replied that she did.

"Well," he said, "it will cost you twenty bucks . . . *no small bills.*"

Ka-*ching*!

tough enough

WHEN CASEY AND COLE WERE STILL LITTLE AND we lived in Dallas, I was out driving with them one day when I noticed two African-American ladies walking down the street, and I casually waved to them.

"Do you know who those ladies are?" Casey asked.

"No, I was just waving to be nice," I told her. "There aren't a whole lot of black people around here, so I waved to acknowledge them and make them feel safe."

"Mom, they weren't black," said Cole, ever the literal little boy. "They were *brown*."

"Yes, I know, but 'black' is what you call people who are our color—black or African American."

"Well, what do you call white people?" Casey asked.

"Caucasian or Anglo," I replied.

"How about peach?" she mused.

What a world it would be if we all saw ourselves and everyone else as peach and chocolate and caramel, right?

My mom has told me that when I was younger I asked her if we were going to stay this color, because I grew up in a neighborhood that was predominantly white. In fact, my sister and I were usually the only black kids in our entire grade school. That demographic didn't change much as I grew up. The only black guy in my high school asked me to homecoming. I thought he was a bit of a jerk, and I knew the feeling was mutual, but we pretended we liked each other so we could go to the dance together. In those days interracial dating was just not something that was going to happen in our neck of the woods.

Although times have changed and interracial dating is more common, Casey and Cole are in a similar situation to mine, as there are few people of color in their school. Many of my friends and acquaintances have questioned why we moved to a small suburban town when we could have made the decision to live in the racially diverse New York City. I chose Picketfenceville not only because it has great schools but also because it felt like home to me. I'm not a big-city girl. I like having a house and a lawn and a backyard for the kids to play in, and in which the dog can chew up my shoes.

So far I don't regret moving there. I feel like my kids have a strong sense of identity based on who we are, and who our family and extended family is. For me, that's who should teach them about their identity—not anyone else. I don't yet feel the need to make a decision based solely on race and move so that my kids can go to a more diverse high school. In fact, that might be more detrimental because their friends are all here, and Casey and Cole are comfortable in their environment. What I will impress upon them is that they can teach people—those who would not normally be exposed to people of a different race—about our values and beliefs.

But that doesn't mean I keep my head in the sand.

Example: I had leased a Mercedes when we'd lived in Dallas, and I no longer needed it once we moved to New York. So I called the dealer in Texas, and he told me to take it to a local dealer. One Saturday we decided to turn the car in and get it over with. Clad in my usual weekend outfit of jeans and a tank top, my hair hidden under a baseball cap and my face devoid of any makeup, I left the house first, with Buff following in his car with Casey and Cole, who were seven and five at the time. Surprise, surprise, Mr. I Don't Need a Map got lost, and I arrived at the dealer first.

When I told the receptionist I was there to bring my car in, she said, in front of everyone else, in a loud, vile tone of voice, "Well, we're not accepting your car on a Saturday."

Taken aback, I asked to speak to her supervisor. Vile employee number two, the general sales manager, came up to me. "She's right—we're not taking it back," he informed me, also in a snooty tone, and loud enough for all to hear.

"I dealt with this already, and was told I could bring the car back here," I said. "Can we go somewhere private to discuss this?"

Without a word he turned on his heel and walked away. I followed him to his office, where he didn't have the basic courtesy to offer me a chair.

"Look," I explained, "I think you guys are treating me like this because I'm dressed down today and I'm African American."

"THAT IS NOT TRUE," he immediately shouted.

Which meant, of course, that it was.

I finally got him to calm down and see my point. At which point Buff showed up, and he let that jerk have it.

They grudgingly took the car back once they realized I had been a regular customer at the Texas branch. Once I was out of that wretched place, I collapsed into a heap of bawling mess in Buff's car. I had never been so humiliated. And as I sat there, sobbing, I could feel two pairs of perplexed and worried little eyes boring into the back of my head.

Later that night I had a long cuddle with Casey and Cole in my bed and explained to them that the reason I'd been crying was that sometimes some people treat other people a certain way based solely on the color of their skin and how they look on the outside. I explained that this wasn't fair and wasn't right, and would never be right, but that it is what it is and this is the world we live in. And the man in the car store had been rude to Mommy because he had judged me based only on how I looked.

Casey started to silently weep, and my sweet Cole's eyes got even bigger than usual, and he choked up, as if he'd swallowed a piece of meat that had a big bone in it. "But why would he do that, Mommy?" he cried. "Why was he so mean?"

What upset me most of all was that I didn't want to have to be the one to explain why racism exists to innocent little children, who should be thinking only about what clothes to put on a doll or where all the LEGO pieces have disappeared to. They shouldn't have to think about why some car sales manager had treated me like dirt. Why should they have to learn about the nastiness of the big, bad world at such a tender age?

I especially worry about this where Cole is concerned. No matter how cute he is as a child, once he grows older, he won't be able to escape the fact that he will always be judged by our society as a black boy and as a black man.

As much as we want to protect our kids from the big, bad world, there's no way to skirt around the tough stuff. I saw this every day from the anchor desk, and am often asked how I feel after I report on a particularly terrible story about a child. Every parent's worst nightmare is that something will happen to his or her child, and I can't help but get twinges of fear when I have to discuss a hurt child, or one who has disappeared or been killed.

And to tell you the truth, before I had kids, those stories never impacted me in the way they do now. I know that being a mother has added a dimension to me as a news anchor that wasn't there before. How could it not?

What's key, for me, is to model appropriate behavior to my own kids. Trust me—I don't let incidents of racism slide by. After the car salesman incident, I wrote a letter to Mercedes-Benz USA telling them in nice, calm language that I know they spend millions of dollars trying to get people like me to buy their cars, but after this I would never consider buying another Mercedes again.

I sent it off with a CC to the rude sales manager. But he didn't apologize. To make matters worse, someone twisted this incident into an item "suitable" for the gossip columns. "Page Six" in the *New York Post* carried a blind item that went something along the lines of: *What television anchor pitched a fit because the dealer wouldn't take her Mercedes back on a busy Saturday?* As a result of the sales manager's reaction to my letter, I felt I had been victimized twice.

When I talk to my kids about tough stuff, I try to use words in a polite way, and I try to avoid little white lies to sugarcoat certain situations. I know that kids have very long memories, and they'll remember what you've said—so these little white lies can backfire in a big way as your kids grow older and are more capable of processing the tough stuff themselves. They'll remember that you didn't trust them enough with the truth.

But how do you prepare your children for something that you know is a major life step, or that is difficult to confront or deal with? Do you just roll with the punches? How do you minimize how evil some people can be without lying about human nature?

I'm the kind of person who finds it hard to hide my stress, although obviously for grown-up-only problems I keep them to myself. When appropriate, I've learned to make my kids be partners in the adventure. We're a family, and we'll tackle whatever we have to deal with as a family.

But that doesn't mean I give the kids equal footing. No way! I give them the vote—but not the veto. I let them be heard, because that validates their fears and feelings, but I will always maintain the power of the veto.

Because the kids know they can talk to me about anything without getting the door slammed in their faces, they are able to confide in me. (Yeah, I know, give it a few years and I will get the door slammed in *my* face!) Casey had a big speech to give at school, and I asked her if she was nervous and she said yes. Then she asked me if I ever got nervous when I had to talk in front of people. I said yes, absolutely. I think that helped her understand that I, too, am human, and even though I have been on TV five days a week, knowing that millions of people are watching me, I still have the same sorts of emotions and anxieties and trepidation that she has about speeches.

What's tricky, though, is knowing when you've strayed

into the Too Much Information Zone and either scared your kids half to death or, in Cole's case, given him lots of great new naughty things to think about so he can try them himself.

This is when the good-enough mother thing kicks in. I make a lot of decisions based on my gut. That's what good-enough mothers do. They listen to their instincts.

Okay, so maybe I'm being a little cuckoo here, as this philosophy might be fine when it comes to managing spats and playdates and how to talk to (or avoid) a teacher, but it's not always the best way to deal with the tough stuff.

And why is that? Because I'm an *emotional* person, that's why! Just ask my husband.

But when I calm down and really listen to my gut with the tough stuff, I feel like I *do* know how to give Casey and Cole the right amount of information. Whatever the issue, if you give kids what they need and speak to them in a way that they understand, you ought to muddle through without a problem. I don't need to go into the mechanics of sexual reproduction when the kids want to know why boys pee standing up, and I don't need to go into all the horrific details about child predators or pedophiles when they're in the news. You don't have to talk down to them or use big, scientific-sounding or confusing words.

And you should never, ever *create* anxiety by saying something like, "Don't worry, honey, everything will be fine." You want a lie detector? Forget about the machine and the wires— hire a child.

Kids have an internal radar that allows them to see right through white lies and soothing platitudes. Trying to shy away from the tough stuff when your kids are small is tantamount to setting yourself up for a very large fall as they grow older.

Chances are good that they'll remember the precise white lie you used as an avoidance technique, and then you'll have to cope with explaining the tough stuff *and* apologizing for lying in the first place.

I also think part of dealing with the tough stuff is teaching your kids how to trust their own instincts. If they feel that something is wrong, it probably *is* wrong. I don't want to be the kind of mom who shuts her kids down by dismissing whatever it is they're telling me. You know, the "Oh, you don't know what you're talking about." Or the "Oh, you don't know what's good for you." Even very small children can be matter-of-factly taught that their private parts are private and that if someone they don't know (or someone they do) tries to touch the child in an inappropriate manner, it's okay for the child to tell that person to stop, and to let the child's parents or teacher know immediately.

I've found that the best time to talk about the tough stuff is usually when everyone is relaxed and not thinking about it. You know, the little-pebbles technique. Throw out a few little pebbles, and you can deal with the ripples. Throw in a big, fat rock and you're going to get wet.

So I'm always on the lookout for opportunities to drop in a few of those little pebbles. Maybe it'll be during dessert, when someone says something about an incident at school. Or when you're in the car and the kids don't have to look you in the eye. Or at the end of the day, when the kids are winding down, are well fed, and they see something on TV.

Once, Casey and Cole were in the kitchen, engrossed in playing, and I was making my usual breakfast-for-dinner meal of mancakes. The TV was on so I could listen to the local news. Without any warning, a segment came on about child predators, with details about a man who'd been preying on ten-year-old girls—the same age as my daughter.

Well, Casey heard this and it was like a dog with a bone—she just wouldn't and couldn't let it go. My stress level rose from zero to sixty, and I tried not to panic about what to say to her, until I realized this was a Teachable Moment. "Listen, if you are ever in a situation like this where somebody touches you inappropriately," I told her, "you need to run and scream and get away. If anyone ever grabs you, you kick and kick and scream and bite and run away. Then let somebody know. Go to somebody you trust, like a policeman or a security guard or someone working in a store. You can always trust a mommy or daddy who is out with their children. Now let's practice our kicking technique."

So we all got down on the floor and started kicking. After a minute we were all laughing, and the tension was defused.

Hopefully the lesson will stick—although, of course I hope like hell they'll never need to use it—but I spent a sleepless night, wondering if I'd said too much, or not enough. On the one hand, you need to plant the seeds because it is a big, bad world out there, but on the other hand, you want to preserve your kids' innocence as long as is humanly possible.

And kids fixate on different dangers. My kids don't like to go downstairs at night because it's dark. I tell them it's okay because this house is protected and nothing bad is going to happen. That's one of my pet phrases: Nothing Bad Is Going to Happen in Our House.

But how can I be so sure? People can trip and fall down a staircase. Wiring can be faulty. Am I promising more than I can deliver?

Another danger they used to fixate on was tornadoes. When we lived in Dallas, tornadoes were not infrequent, and the sight of them in *The Wizard of Oz* was good for a few nightmares. Thanks a lot, Miss Gulch!

So when we moved to Westchester County, I told Casey and Cole that this wasn't tornado country and that they'd be safe from tornadoes here because they didn't form in this kind of terrain. Well, guess what? Last summer there was a tornado, not too far from the house. I had some explaining to do. "Well," I said, pointing to the headlines, "they did say this was a very rare event. It shouldn't happen again."

"Yeah, right," said Cole.

Dang—my credibility was shot!

As for drugs and smoking and drinking, our school district is pretty good about dealing with information about bad habits, but of course it's up to parents to drive the lessons home. Neither Buff nor I smoke, and so when Casey and Cole see someone smoke, they know it's disgusting and they're suitably repulsed. I'll usually add a comment or two about how smokers' lungs are going to look like the inside of an ashtray, and so far that has done the trick. Luckily, we haven't had to talk much about drugs.

Yet. I know that's coming. And coming soon. I hope I'm ready when the kids are teens and their peers are starting to experiment with substances that you'd rather not think about.

When it comes to drinking, Buff and I do like a glass with dinner, and that's that. Because we drink in moderation and in such a casual way, I hope that our kids see alcohol as something to savor in small doses, not abuse.

Although Casey and Cole do have a good role model of

appropriate drinking for pleasure, not for sport, Cole is at an age when he's fascinated by excessive drinkers. One of his favorite new phrases is "He's *drunk*."

"How do you even know what that means?" I asked him the first time he said that. ("How do you even know what that means?" is one of my most-quoted sentences where Cole is concerned!) "Who have you ever seen who's been drunk?"

He mentioned someone from some TV show, and I relaxed. Then I seized the opportunity to talk to him about how he can make decisions about this himself when he's twenty-one, and how I dealt with the pressures my peers put on me to have a few drinks with them when they were teenagers.

"Oh," he said, "you mean when they were *drunk*."

# of super-moms and halloweenies

WHEN I TOLD SOME OF MY FRIENDS THAT I was going to write a chapter about the perfectionist, confident, superior, my-kid-is-smarter-than-yours-and-always-will-be-even-if-you-are-on-TV-and-writing-a-book-and-I-haven't-had-a-job-since-I-got-married-at-twenty-three-to-that-insider-trader-with-a-silver-spoon kind of mom, looks of sheer horror crossed my friends' faces.

"Are you crazy?" they asked me. "No one in the PTA will ever talk to you again!"

"Yes, they will," I replied. "I'm writing about *composites*. You know, *archetypes*. I'm not mentioning anyone by name. It's not about *them*."

My girlfriends rolled their eyes.

"Just wait till you get snubbed at Starbucks," they said.

Such is the power of these women that the mere hint that I might be addressing them instantly set my girlfriends off in a paroxysm of apprehension, swatting away at those nagging little gnats of self-doubt, which always seem to come a-flyin' whenever one of the species of females known and feared worldwide as the Dreaded Super-Moms lands nearby.

Dreaded Super-Moms have a knack for effortlessly parallel parking (into the spot you were impatiently waiting for, while you are looking your worst) in their custom-detailed SUVs, with an air of supreme calm and confidence, dressed to the nines in their custom-tailored snow gear, with freshly blown-out hair, and teeth that have just been brightened to pearly perfection.

Dreaded Super-Moms exude a heady perfume, with a note of "I know more than you and I am better than you" laid atop a base of "my kids are better than yours." In their neatly ordered minds—unlike mine, where the synapses fire in rapid patterns of emotionality—everything has to be done *just so*. They are the judge, jury, and defense team. They make the rules. Never mind that they forget to tell nonmembers of the Dreaded Super-Mom Club what those rules are. If either you or your child does not fit into their preconceived idea of appropriate behavior, then you are off the list.

The Dreaded Super-Moms have a particular knack for showing up whenever we're least likely to be in the mood to deal with their noblesse oblige. This means we may encounter them while, for example, grumpily grocery shopping. There they airily float by us in the supermarket, their carts laden with kale and kumquats, while ours are loaded with sugar pops cereal and frozen pizza. Their children are quiet and ever-so-well-behaved, while Casey is cramming a handful of Pringles (from the can I haven't paid for yet) into her mouth and Cole is sheepishly denying that he just broke the jar of spaghetti sauce in aisle six when his Heelys refused to heel.

Yep, it would be easy for me to develop the same inferiority complex some of my girlfriends have when watching all the Dreaded Super-Moms. But I don't, for one simple reason: I Don't Care.

That's my standby mantra, which you already know is a handy-dandy, all-purpose state of mind that every good-enough mother should do her utmost to hone to perfection.

As I've said already, for years I worried about what people thought of me—not just the Dreaded Super-Moms but also other people with whom I came into contact. Well, guess what?

Worrying about what other people think of me is a total waste of time. Not my bosses and colleagues and family and close friends, of course. But people who have no real bearing on how I run my life or how I look or feel.

Ignore the behavior that you want extinguished and it should go away.

And if it doesn't, well, you know my mantra. I Don't Care!

I have a theory about the Dreaded Super-Mom, whose sole purpose in life seems to be to make others feel less accomplished and somehow lacking in whatever area she decided upon that morning as she was patting her perfectly glowing hair into submission. My theory is that the Dreaded Super-Moms are emotional bullies, the adult incarnation of the mean girls who tortured so many of us in middle school and high school.

Back in those best-forgotten days when I was a teen, the mean girls ran the cliques, and I knew from the minute I walked into school that I wouldn't be welcome in them (too tall, too skinny, too tomboyish, too funny, too smart, too much of a wallflower, too black). You either wore Jordache jeans or you didn't. My mother's face when she saw the price tag on the pair of Jordache jeans I begged her to buy me was a real big clue that I was not going to be gloating over my denim-clad butt anytime soon.

Like most other teens, I wanted to be popular in high school, but it was just not in the cards. I never bothered trying out for the cheerleading squad, spiritual home of the mean girls, because I couldn't do the splits, and you know you can't be a cheerleader if you don't do splits. Instead, I tried out for the flag team—not the team with the cute tiny little flags that were easy to manage, mind you, but the team with the HTM (hard-to-manage) big flags. It wouldn't even have been a huge step up if I'd made the team. In my school the pecking order was cheerleaders, drill team, small flag team, HTM big flag team, and all the rest, who were so hopelessly uncoordinated they were given study hall instead of gym. I was confident. There were seven spots on the HTM big flag team, and only eight people tried out. The odds were really good, but—you guessed it—I didn't make it.

I am an HTM big-flag-team reject!

And what pissed me off was that I was strong and fast and coordinated. Of course I could twirl a flag—I could twirl a flag on one leg, blindfolded.

But the mean girls didn't like me, so I was an HTM big-flag-team reject.

I got upset, of course, and this could have done a real number on my already low self-esteem. I could have thrown myself a big ol' pity party. Instead, I clearly remember my mom sitting down with me and saying, "They don't know what they're doing. You are really very beautiful. Don't worry about what people think—just be yourself. Life doesn't begin and end with the flag team. You're destined for much bigger and better things. For some of these girls, high school's gonna be the high point of their lives, and it'll be all downhill from there. You're gonna be a late bloomer, and you'll show them. Just remember that."

So I dried my tears and had a long, hard think about why I was so upset. And then the little lightbulb went off, and I felt about a hundred pounds lighter. The stupid, selfish cliquishness of the mean girls had suddenly freed me from the weight of trying to please and impress them. I mean, why should I bother dealing with people whose opinion was, actually, meaningless? After all, I knew that I'd been the best one to try out for the dorky big flag team, and my rejection had not been about my skills—but about someone else's preconceived notion of what they'd wanted and who they could hurt.

Once I realized I'd never be a member of the in crowd, I said the mantra to myself, for the very first time: I Don't Care.

It sounded really good. It felt even better.

I said it again, realizing that I was not going to let anyone make me feel inadequate.

And then I got comfortable being *myself*.

I know how lucky I am to have a mother who loved and believed in me, unconditionally, and who insisted that I be myself, and showed me that I was special. This support and encouragement was especially important after an incident that became a turning point in my young life.

When I was in fourth grade, age ten (the same age Casey is now), I was riding my bike in our nice neighborhood one day when I saw a man, who was directly opposite me, walking down the street.

"Hey, you nigger!" he called out.

All these years later, the memory is as fresh as if it had happened yesterday. I felt as if I'd just ridden my bike straight into a brick wall. In fact, I almost did fall off, so shocked was I by the hatred I'd heard in that man's voice. For the first time in my life I felt that I was different, and that I had been cruelly singled out by a stranger solely for something as superficial as the color of my skin.

I rode home, terribly upset and crying my eyes out, and my mom sat down with me and waited until I was calm.

"Listen to me," she said, looking right into my eyes. "You *belong* here. You have a *right* to be here. Don't let anyone tell you differently. You're *you*, and you're *special*. What anyone you don't know says or thinks about you means *nothing*."

I don't think I ever loved my mom before as much as I did right that instant.

So where the Dreaded Super-Moms and their sense of entitlement are concerned, they really don't bother me. I know where I belong (even if they don't). And the point that I try my utmost to get across to my kids is that they, too, have a right to occupy their space on this planet, and what anyone they don't know says or thinks about them means *nothing*.

It's hard not to think about entitlement and superiority on the rare occasions when I drive my kids to school. One of the few perks of my middle-of-the-night pickup time for work is that I'm usually spared what should earn combat pay for mothers who have to face this on a daily basis—the Carpool Gauntlet.

The Carpool Gauntlet is serious business. If you mess up, make one wrong turn, or (horrors!) cut someone off, you're immediately exiled to Bad Mommy Land. Worse, you run the risk of having your children ostracized because their idiot mother couldn't follow the cones.

Anyway, because I navigate the Carpool Gauntlet so infrequently, I always seem to forget where I am and what I'm supposed to do, and once, I inadvertently cut off (horrors!) one of the Dreaded Super-Moms. Mea culpa, and all that. But she then proceeded to bestow upon me a glance so withering— really, how dare I intrude on her space and innate entitlement to it?—and so vastly, ridiculously, and disproportionately hostile compared to the offense at hand. The intent was to shrivel anyone other than a good-enough mother, who is protected from such withering looks by the potency of her mantras.

Well, kiss my bumper!

As I drove away, I couldn't help but muse on what makes the Dreaded Super-Moms tick. My curiosity came more from a culturally motivated journalist's point of view than from any deep, dark interest as to the inner workings of their psyches. I decided long ago that they are the adult incarnation of the Mean Girls I knew so well in high school.

Funny, isn't it, how you never really get out of high school?

Now, as grown women, who are the Mean-Girls-turned-superior trying to impress? Why is it so important for them to bask in their alleged superiority? I mean, raising children isn't exactly some crazy race where at the finish line, when your kids are eighteen and about to leave the nest, you get an award because your kid wore the Miss Sixty jeans, or got into Harvard, or whatever it'll be that's on the top of their list. For me, that's not what parenting—or life—is about. It's about not making yourself crazy or making your kids crazy.

I'd like to believe that all moms are doing the best they can. My own philosophy is that we all want to matter in this life. No matter what it is you've chosen to do with your life, what you make your mark doing, you just want to count. With the Dreaded Super-Moms, I don't see the competitiveness so much as a contest with their peers but as a sort of competition with *themselves*. Lots of them quit high-powered, satisfying jobs to raise their kids, and they can't help clicking back into bark mode. Their children become their jobs—the vessels of all their hopes and dreams.

And God help the child of a Dreaded Super-Mom if the child doesn't deliver.

I wonder if the Dreaded Super-Moms have, perhaps, just a little too much time on their hands than is good for them. It's amazing how little time you have to micromanage everyone else's lives when you have a life of your own. I think this is one of the reasons the Dreaded Super-Moms become hyperinvolved in school activities. They need the control; they need the power; and they need bragging rights that their offspring has a parent who is *so* visible and making *such* a difference!

This attitude can really be upsetting to good-enough mothers. I have a friend, a working woman with an extremely successful career and a job she loves, who went to school and introduced herself to the teachers and other parents. As she walked away from the group, she heard one of the Dreaded Super-Moms say, "Don't worry. We will never see her again."

Well, my friend told me she went home and cried all day. There she was, trying to do what she felt was right for her kids while trying to remain true to herself, and some woman who didn't have to work—because she'd married someone who did work—was judging her. *Walk a mile in our shoes*, I wanted to say to those Dreaded Super-Moms. *Maybe our jobs are really important to us, but that doesn't mean our kids are less important.*

In my mind, it's crucial to be a well-rounded person, and to do that I have to get out of the house; I have to work; and I have no patience for those who pass judgment on someone else's needs and circumstances. My identity isn't solely invested in or dependent upon my children. So when somebody makes a critical comment about Cole's, um, *exuberance*, I know that it isn't about me and my alleged failings—it's about the fact that Cole is, um, *exuberant*!

Actually, the entire premise of this book is about admitting that it's okay to be imperfect, to be good enough. In fact, you *should* be imperfect for your children, because you don't want them to grow up in a world where everything seems perfect. What kind of world is that?

If my kids are going to be disappointed, let me be the first on the list to disappoint them. That way we can tackle the disappointment together, figure out what didn't work, and move on. Successful parenting is about giving your kids the tools to cope. If they get all the way through their childhoods without having a single disappointment, which is highly unlikely, what will they do when they're in college and get their first, savage disappointment? How will they have the skills to cope?

Don't tell me that these Dreaded Super-Moms' kids aren't saying to themselves, on some level, "Please, Mom, can't you just dial it back a notch?"

As much as you might want to do everything for your kids

because it's easier in the short term, you just can't. A good-enough mother doesn't want to. She knows that the shortest path between two points is a straight line—one that you draw and follow yourself. Oh, sure, you can help your kids walk that line with some (or a lot of) gentle encouragement, but what's crucial is for your child to discover his or her own strengths and to cultivate his or her imagination along the way.

If you walk the walk for them, they'll go from *A* to *Z* without the rest of the alphabet holding them up. And then they'll fall.

Take a walk in the toddler toy aisles and you'll see how many of the must-haves of the season are the kinds of toys that walk the walk for kids. They're tie-ins to a noisy movie, or they say and do only prescribed things—in essence, they're doing the playing *for* the children, instead of *with* them. And I think we all know that kids often have more fun playing with the boxes the toys come in than with the toys themselves. The box has limitless possibilities. It can be anything a child wants it to be. A battery-powered superhero cannot.

A walk through the toddler aisle last Halloween gave me a bit of a shock. Not only were the toys garish and predictable but an entire section had also been set up with ornate Halloween costumes (with matching ornate price tags) for toddlers (and babies!), costumes that would have been more appropriate for the Broadway stage than for a two-hour trick-or-treat spree.

I'm used to seeing many older children in the ornate costumes, but that's because Halloween seems to have turned into the warm-up to Christmas, what with the over-the-top light displays and the sheer amount of merchandise for parties and backyard graveyards. I mean, when I was a kid, we painted a sheet to be a ghost and collected candy in an old pillowcase. The thought of buying a costume instead of making your own was inconceivable.

Now, on the other hand, Halloween has become *the* holiday where the Dreaded Super-Moms can really shine. It's nonsectarian. Children are meant to be seen and admired and congratulated. What better opportunity than to outfit the little ones in costumes designed by Karl Lagerfeld, accessorized with Gucci candy bags?

My kids don't expect the ornate getups, as they know that for me the costume thing is as perplexing as the what's-for-dinner question, because I'm not great at conceptualizing how to construct a costume (too much like math), and I can't sew.

However, I am a whiz with the hot glue gun.

So the kids and I turn the what'll-I-wear-for-Halloween costume gig into a family affair. Since I've made it clear that purchasing ornate costumes is out of the question, Casey and Cole have lots of fun coming up with new ideas for costumes they can put together themselves.

Luckily, we always had great guests come on *The Early Show* in the weeks leading up to Halloween, who have costume ideas I'd never think of in a gazillion years. Several years ago one of our guest costume experts showed us how to make a cow costume. She took a pair of white pants and a white shirt and hot-glued patches of black and a tail onto them. I thought, *Hey, wait a minute, I can do that.*

But then I didn't have to. That lovely lady took pity on me and gave me the costume! That year, Cole was a cow. And he loved it.

And Halloween is the one day of the year when the candy is allowed to flow, and so we concentrate on the treating rather than on the dress-up, especially because I have no intention of entering the Dreaded Super-Mom My Costume Is More Expensive Than Yours contest. To make Halloween even more fun for me, I finally figured out an infallible method of besting the Dreaded Super-Moms.

Our community has few sidewalks, and the homes are spread out, so it's hard (and dangerous) for the kids to trick-or-treat the way I did as a kid, going door-to-door to closely spaced houses in the neighborhood. Instead, the merchants in our compact downtown give kids an opportunity to destroy as much tooth enamel as possible by doling out fistfuls of candy.

Anyway, the way I bested the Super-Moms was by first racing home from work so I could get to the school in time to pick up Casey and Cole. When I arrived at school, all the parents were already there. Their ultimate goal was the same as mine: to race into town and get as much candy as possible. But they milled around, showing off the designer costumes they'd so painstakingly bought and put together, getting ready to put them on their kids and then take off.

But, oh no, not me. I was *so* much smarter.

"Come on, come on," I said to Casey and Cole, grabbing them by the hands. "We gotta go, we gotta go, we gotta *go!*"

We ran out to the car, Casey and Cole practically out of breath and exchanging what's-gotten-into-her-now glances.

"Jump in," I blared, my voice rising. "You can change into your costumes in the car."

They did, and we made it into town before anyone else. Casey and Cole got a ton of candy before all the other kids did. And if you ask them, they'll tell you it was one of the best afternoons they've ever had.

So what if the Dreaded Super-Moms thought I was off my rocker.

Repeat after me: I Don't Care.

And here's what I don't understand about Halloween: Why is it so important for the Dreaded Super-Moms to have their kids be designer-clad fairy princesses or emperors or ninja turtles? Why are these moms so afraid of showing a little imagination and encouraging their kids to be peacocks or Balinese temple dancers or someone else who would need a handmade costume?

If Cole wants to be a cow, then I'm gonna let him be a cow, as long as I don't have to sew the costume myself.

So the next time one of the Dreaded Super-Moms does her utmost to make the rest of us feel less than adequate, I tell myself not only that I don't care but also that I *am* a Super-Mom.

After all, I am a *mom*.

And my kids think I'm pretty *super*.

another note from mrs. henry

THROUGHOUT MY CAREER I'VE INTERVIEWED many influential people, but I was never more nervous than I was the time I sat across from Cole's second-grade teacher, Mrs. Henry, at a parent-teacher conference and asked, "How's Cole listening?"

She said, "Not well. If he doesn't improve, perhaps he might need to repeat the second grade."

The room began to spin and I felt sick to my stomach.

Mrs. Henry, in her infinite wisdom, had come up with a plan to modify some of Cole's "undesirable behaviors" and "listening challenges," as she put it. I didn't have the heart to tell her that Mrs. Magenta, his first-grade teacher, had already tried to do the same. The only behavior she'd been able to extinguish was Cole's tying his shoelaces together and hopping off to the lunchroom.

Part of my problem with Cole is that trying to discipline him is like trying to discipline myself. I listen to his teachers recite the litany of his misdeeds, and it's all I can do to repress the chuckles—because, sadly, it's *so me!*

Like the time my son, in full class-clown mode, wrote a sign and then held it over his head. The sign read I'M DEMENTED.

Naturally, my first thought was: *Did he spell it right?*

Second thought: *How does he know what that means?*

Third thought: *That's really funny, and I hate to admit it, but it is true a lot of the time!*

Cole defies authority for the simplest of reasons: Because he can. Buff is not exactly my partner in discipline when it comes to this issue. He's not one to worry that we have a baby derelict on our hands. In fact, Buff's typical response to one of Cole's escapades is to say something like, "Oh, Cole's always going to be a nonconformist."

Hey, thanks, pal. Idi Amin was a nonconformist. So was Joseph Stalin.

No, I need Buff to help me help Cole to conform . . . at least until we leave Mrs. Henry's class. We've got to nip this in the bud, because I don't want to raise a second-grade despot. Sure, I'm all about letting Cole express his individuality, but there's not enough Clairol at Rite Aid to cover all the gray hairs that boy is giving me.

Buff's response to my distress?

"He'll grow out of it."

I began to think that Cole wasn't going to grow out of it, as he was having so much trouble concentrating. Just to be on the safe side, I made an appointment with a neuropsychologist to rule out any sort of ADHD or other learning disability. When I told Cole I was taking him to a brain doctor, he with wide-eyed wonder asked, "Are they gonna cut my head open?"

Much to his chagrin, I had to tell him no.

Casey, my sweet people pleaser, has always been a model student. She knows what I expect and what her teachers expect, and she does it without fail. If she falls short, as all kids sometimes do, I gently let her know, and she'll punish herself more than I ever could.

Once, when she was trying to memorize her lines for the school play, she was having such a tough time that it sent her into a quick tailspin of upset and frustration.

I sat down with her and taught her a useful trick. "If you break it down and take it one line at a time, you'll be fine. This is what I do when I have to memorize anything."

She looked skeptical, but after less than an hour of studying, she had it. I could literally see her get all pumped up because she was so proud of herself.

Because Casey has always been such a good student, I am always happy when she hands me a note from one of her teachers. They invariably say something nice.

Cole, not surprisingly, has gotten a stack of notes, which is now practically as tall as the Eiffel Tower.

I was perfectly blasé the first time I got a note from one of Cole's teachers.

He was only three.

See, I sent Casey and Cole to a Montessori preschool when we lived in Dallas. Casey positively blossomed in that environment, since she's a motivated self-starter who also has no problem taking direction. Cole needed more structure. For Casey it is reward enough to finish a task or a project or a good book. Cole will protest every step of the way.

Children are individuals, and as such can have very different learning styles—which means that you have to approach their schoolwork and progress without comparisons and with an open mind. Siblings often loathe the continual comparisons to each other's intellectual strengths and learning abilities, and you need to be careful to make sure you're not judging one against the other.

As a result, I did have a lot of sleepless nights wondering if I should keep Cole in the same school as Casey, as the Montessori method played more to her strengths than to his. Ultimately, in retrospect, I don't think it was the wrong choice to keep Cole there, even with their specific behavioral approach, and even though the notes from the teachers kept arriving with increasing frequency. When I look at the choices I've made in my life, I don't think of any of them as *mistakes*. I think of them as *learning opportunities*.

This is part of the essence of the good-enough mother's philosophy. I could have taken a different path to be where I am today, but all the things that I've ever done and learned have combined to make me who I am. Yep, I'm the sum total of all those experiences, good and bad. Voilà! Here I am!

So, with respect to kids and school, I've always felt that if you start off steering down one path and get lost, you switch and go in another direction. I'm a living example of this. I spent four years in college studying psychology, certain that I wanted to be a therapist. At the time, I never dreamed that I'd wind up as a broadcast journalist instead. Did I regret the four long years getting into debt as a psych student? Hell, no! It ended up leading me where I needed to be, and it allowed me to meet people and to learn researching skills that became invaluable in my new career.

Still, if you have a stressful job and the kids are having trouble at school and you're just *tired*, it's very easy (and totally understandable) to fall into a trap of complacency and to become paralyzed by procrastination. (Or to do the kids' home-work for them.) One thing I've learned is that you can't steer a still ship. You've got to figure out some way to fill the sails with wind and set yourself back on course.

In other words, as the Nike ads say, you've gotta just do it.

What works for me is to set small goals for myself that are easily attainable. Don't expect to make sweeping changes in all aspects of your life at once.

Certainly, don't stop dreaming. Don't laugh, but I often think about becoming a doctor. Okay, I know I'd have a real problem making it through medical school with my lack of math skills, and I would be several decades older than most of the students, but, well, so what? I could do it if I really put my mind to it. Or, at the very least, I could take a class or two to see if the dream were at all realistic.

Of course, I'm the first to admit I don't always follow my own advice. When it came to meeting with Mrs. Henry, just doing it was not something that came easily. How I wish Cole had been as terrified of Mrs. Henry as I was! She falls into the "take no prisoners" category of teachers. Every time I got yet another note from her, my stomach started churning.

Not all the notes were bad, though. When she and I worked really hard together to give Cole a behavior chart—spelling out exactly the things he needed to do and what the consequences would be if he didn't do them—Mrs. Henry was stunned into shocked surprise. Yet she was quick with the praise. In fact, one note practically said, *Omigod, Cole was so good today! That goes to show you that he does have it in him.*

He just needed the right motivation.

Back then, positive reinforcement was easy. A big kiss and

hug and effusive praise were more than enough. Now, of course, Cole wants money. I tell him to forget about it, that a kiss and a hug or a high five—as well as acknowledgment of how proud I am of his efforts—will have to do.

Well, just as I was basking in satisfaction, along came another note from Mrs. Henry a scant two days later.

I think we need to have a conference at your earliest convenience, it said.

The morning of our designated meeting, my three alarms went off at 3:40, 3:45, and 3:50. With each one came a growing sense of dread. Not because I had a long day ahead of me. Not because I had too many bills and money was tight that month.

Nope, it was because I had my meeting with Mrs. Henry at four p.m.

I threw off the covers and stumbled to the shower, hoping that the steam would start to chase the fog from my sleep-deprived brain. I mentally reviewed my on-air interviews for that morning, including a chat with Attorney General Alberto Gonzales. All of a sudden my eyes snapped open and my heart leapt into my throat. Omigod, THE READING LOG! On top of having a meeting with Mrs. Henry, I'd forgotten to sign Cole's reading log!

Crap. Just what I needed. Not only was I about to be reamed by Mrs. Henry for all my mistakes as a parent to my rambunctious son, but I couldn't even manage something as basic as the daily log, something I should have been able to do almost in my sleep. Forget about trying to juggle—I couldn't even get one ball up in the air.

And I also knew that Mrs. Henry would always take

priority over the attorney general—if only because I wouldn't have to see *him* at the next parent-teacher conference!

I thought about handling my Mrs. Henry phobia the way I used to handle things I didn't want to deal with, back when I was in grade school. I'd shut my eyes real tight and hold my breath until I was light-headed. I wished I could still do that, but moms don't have the luxury of wishing their anxieties away. They need to confront them, and move on.

As always happens when you're dreading something, the day flew by. Before I knew it, it was late afternoon. I made my way to the school. By that point all the buses were long gone. In fact, everyone seemed long gone. It was eerily quiet, like in one of those bad sci-fi flicks where the aliens have come and obliterated everyone and all that's left are three pieces of paper blowing around on the playground.

Slowly, slowly, I forced one foot in front of the other, down the long hallway to Mrs. Henry's class, the amplified sound of my high-heeled boots reverberating in a thudding echo. The only thing missing was the jailer who yells "Dead man walking" as the prisoner is escorted to the death chamber.

When I finally dragged myself into the classroom, Mrs. Henry's greeting was warm and inviting. She and I took seats at opposite ends of the table. I settled into a chair, trying to get comfortable, which was nearly impossible, with half my adult-size butt sliding over the edge of the child-size seat.

I realized how hard it is to be authoritative when your knees are hovering near your boobs. It's comical that standing my ground in all my years in the media and with the thousands of people I've interviewed meant nothing in Mrs. Henry's classroom. I felt instantly transported back to the second grade.

After a minute of small talk Mrs. Henry zoomed in for the kill. The real reason I was there was because Cole was the class cutup. She ran down her litany of Cole complaints: He's easily distracted, then he distracts others. He fidgets. He doesn't hang up his coat. He doesn't finish his work in the allotted time. He doesn't keep his eyes on the speaker. He claims he can't tie his shoes (he can), and he got the second-lowest score on the math test.

In other words, he was acting like a typical boy.

I listened. And nodded. And then—you know the feeling— suddenly there was more water in my eyes than usual. That little voice in my head started repeating, *You will not cry, you will not cry, you will not cry* . . . OH, NO . . . I *was* crying.

I was feeling utterly inadequate as a mom, since what I'd been doing with Cole at home clearly wasn't good enough, *and* I was displaying my vulnerability in front of Mrs. Henry. I felt like a complete failure.

Let's just say that Cole and I had a very long talk when I got home.

On the other hand, I can't help but wonder if, in the long run, he'll be easier to parent than Casey. With Cole, what you see is what you get. He's all there. He's letting it all hang out.

And he acts the same when he plays games. Last time the whole family was on vacation, we all trooped over to a minia- ture golf course for a few rounds. Cole went first, standing in a way that would have driven Tiger Woods to whack a few into the rough.

"Take your time, Cole," I suggested. "Try to line up your shots."

He glanced over at me with a swift scowl, then stood the way he wanted.

"I know what I'm doing," he said.

Then he said it another dozen times—and I have to confess that his crazy stance worked eight out of those twelve times.

Well, yours truly got a powerful lesson in keeping her big ol' yap shut, because even though Cole was only eight at the time, he did know—in his own way—what he was doing. And he had (and still has) the confidence to pull it off.

And I also got a lesson in learning how to let go. It wasn't as though his life had been in jeopardy—it was a *game*. What mattered was his having fun, and learning how to play.

He did both.

I have to admit, the lesson for me was to trust that my kids instinctively know what they're doing—up to a point, of course. As long as they're not juggling with sharp knives or stealing the car keys to go for a joyride, I think moms should at least let their children try something their own way, trusting their own instincts as a good-enough mother trusts hers, before insisting that they conform to the rules of the miniature golf course. Then, together, everyone will be able to find the best way to learn—and in the process we might just come up with a wonderful new way that makes life (and miniature golf) more fun for us all.

flunking out of PTA

LIKE MANY OTHER MOMS, I'M NOT THRILLED when I'm in the mom spotlight. Even though I'm comfortable on national television, and often give speeches and presentations to huge crowds of strangers, no audience has ever been tougher than Cole's classmates the day I had to cook for his kindergarten class.

All the moms had to cook one of their kids' favorite dishes, as part of Show and Share Month. So I decided to make my infamous mancakes, which you'll recall are minipancakes studded with ever-healthful chocolate chips and made even more nutritious by being smothered in whipped cream straight from the nozzle.

Cream is dairy, and dairy has calcium, right?

I figured I'd made mancakes at least 568 times before being invited to Cole's kindergarten class. But as forty eyes turned expectantly to me, and I stood before the box of pancake mix and cups of water on a small crayon-encrusted table, I broke out in a cold sweat. Let's just say that my acknowledged handicaps in the kitchen do not make me a Julia Child manqué. I know my limitations!

Hands fumbling, pancake mix spilling onto the table, water spilling, I finally managed to scrape it all together and cook the mancakes without burning them all.

Never again, I swore.

Nearly as nerve-racking are the preparations necessary to celebrate birthdays in the classroom. At Casey and Cole's school, all the moms are expected to volunteer in the classroom the day of their kids' birthdays, bringing cupcakes (baked from scratch, natch, and decorated with flawless swirls of piped frosting) and good cheer.

Why, oh why, wasn't Cole born in late summer . . . when school is *out*?

When Cole was about to turn seven, he announced that I had to bring doughnuts to his class. Just when I was about to heave a sigh of relief at the thought of being spared the hand-beaten buttercream, Cole informed me that his birthday doughnuts couldn't be just *any* doughnuts. Heavens no—that would have been too easy!

Cole's doughnuts had to be in the shape of a number seven. A classmate's mother had brought in seven-shaped birthday doughnuts a few weeks before, which meant Cole had been harping on the seven-shaped doughnuts ever since.

In order to silence the nagging, finding the seven-shaped doughnuts became Mission Improbable. With the precision of a platoon commander prepping for night maneuvers, I phoned several local doughnut chains until I found the one that could deal in sevens. Dutifully, I called the week before to make sure we had the order in. I called the day before to make sure the doughnuts would be at the shop on time. And I called the morning of the party, just to, well, just to make sure all systems were go.

I canceled my appointments that day and pulled into the doughnut store parking lot at 12:42 p.m., humming a happy tune. At 12:43, you'd have thought the noise emanating from inside the doughnut store was the result of an ox being disemboweled.

The seven-shaped doughnuts had disappeared.

Not only had they disappeared but the pimple-encrusted eighteen-year-old store manager could not even tell me where they were. My blood pressure soared past its normal 120 over 70 as I tried to explain why we could not let my son down. Oh, and don't think I didn't offer to try to cook the dang things myself right there (expert chef that I am), but that was a no go, because the doughnuts were all made at another location and trucked to each store.

I was screwed. But the blubbering tears that ensued were the result of knowing how disappointed Cole would be.

Eventually we found out what had happened: Someone who had a kid celebrating an eighth birthday had come in, and my order of sevens had mistakenly been given to her. At that point I had three choices: I could fly to the grocery store and pick up something else (couldn't do that, had just five minutes to get to the school), show up empty-handed (guaranteed to leave Cole and me in hysterics), or show up with a bunch of doughnuts shaped like eights and tell Cole I'd done my best.

After a deep, cleansing breath I took the eights, much to the relief of the terrified store manager. When I got to class, I explained to Cole and everyone else what had happened. Think they cared?

Not even a little bit. You know why?

Because they got to eat doughnuts in class.

And Cole loved it because his mother had taken the time to do something special for him.

At this same school all parents are required to volunteer for events other than birthday celebrations at least twice a year. Whenever I can, I'll go into Casey's and Cole's classrooms and read, or do projects, or bring in cupcakes. Plus, every year at the Halloween festival I'm a fortune-teller and Buff is a mad scientist. The first year, when we didn't really know the protocol of the party, we thought everyone would be dressed up. Well, no one else was dressed up—and there I was with the long black wig and a bandana.

Then there was the day I volunteered to be a class parent for the second-grade field trip, accompanying Cole's class on an expedition to a rocky beach at a Connecticut state park.

In just one short afternoon I gained newfound respect for Mrs. Henry. God love the woman. I don't know how long she's been teaching, and I guess I may have been less than understanding when she sent home note after note about my little angel Cole, but all the bricks fell into place after that windy afternoon.

Each parent chaperone was given a group of kids to watch. While other parents had three or four children, I had only Cole and one other boy to supervise. The none-too-subtle message was that Cole might physically be one child, but his activity level is the equivalent of three or four.

I'll spare you the details of Cole's charmingly uncontrolled romping on the beach. But with the hot sun and the sand crabs and the sand in the sandwiches, after only about twenty minutes I was ready to go home and have a stiff drink.

I can still hope that his natural exuberance might be successfully channeled into performing. Cole is a natural-born ham who never saw a camera he didn't want to mug for, or a stage he didn't want to hog.

Which brings me to school plays. Interesting how they can have such a potent effect on moms, both good and bad. You can't help but burst with pride at your kids up there on the stage, knowing how hard they worked to memorize lines and blocking—working together with classmates with varying levels of skill and natural stage fright at appearing before a large crowd.

But at the same time, you wish that some of the other moms (usually of the Dreaded Super-Mom variety) weren't quite so heavily invested in having their kids be not only better than yours but also the very best in the entire school.

I find this attitude troubling, as we should be enjoying the school plays solely for what they are. Obviously, not every child can have a speaking part. Few have naturally gorgeous pitch-perfect voices that make *Annie's* "Tomorrow" sound like a ballad instead of a chorus of alley cats in heat. And, most important, school plays should be about the *kids*. About their cuteness and their hard work. The plays aren't about the parents.

I have as yet been unable to broach this sensitive topic with any of the Dreaded Super-Moms. Not that I want to. But I do feel for their kids, and it's a really potent reminder to me to relax and enjoy my children for who they are—not shining stars on a stage who'll someday be thanking me in their Tony Award and Oscar speeches, but kids who are sweetly, sanely, and blessedly normal.

What I do lose sleep over, however, is being able to get to the plays on time. My kids do not expect accolades for their performances, but they do expect acknowledgment in the form of a motherly butt firmly placed in a seat in the auditorium. It's just my luck that plays are usually scheduled for days when I find it impossible to leave work early. I usually have to race into the school auditorium, still with my TV face and wardrobe on. So I look like a professional while trying to not clobber most of the moms who've arrived two hours early to block off entire rows of seats for all their relatives, friends, neighbors, employees, and former Sunday school teachers.

We take school plays *very* seriously in my neck of the woods.

Once, Cole was assigned the role of a sperm whale (no laughing) in his class play. We worked so hard together on his lines (Did you know a sperm whale eats krill? Do you care?), and I was deeply invested in his performance. Well, it took weeks of begging and finagling to secure the special permission to leave the show early so I could race back to see my baby sperm whale discuss delightful, delectable krill.

But, of course, Murphy's Law was in full effect as traffic came to an utter standstill in Manhattan. This was compounded by the fact that the man driving me home that day was literally 198 years old. Anything remotely over the forty-nine miles per hour mark was, in his mind, like moving at the speed of sound.

My anxiety grew with each passing minute and reluctant mile, until it finally dawned on me that I might not make it. This was just not good enough for this good-enough mother. I *had* to make it. I could *not* let my son down. So, first I tried to gently prod the elderly gent, which soon gave way to "YOU'VE REALLY GOT TO STEP ON IT!" and a little bit more of the screaming-type comments.

Finally I arrived at the school with one minute to spare. After jumping out of the car, I raced for the cafeteria, which was where I'd been told the play was being put on. I was greeted by empty chairs and tables. Now, you have to envision this sight: Me dressed in my trim, tailored suit, in a full-on sprint in high heels, clickity-clacking in complete panic through the hallways. By that time, I could no longer form a coherent sentence, much less give real thought as to where I was going. So I ran into the wrong classroom. When I arrived at the right classroom (the same one Cole had been in since the beginning of the school year), all the little mammals were finished and the parents were applauding their performance. I stood there, chest heaving, heart breaking, doing a terrible job of holding back the tears. All of a sudden, like linebackers on the fifty-yard line, parents formed a protective circle around me, patting my back, handing me a tissue, and telling me it was all right and to not let Cole see me crying.

This story does have a happy ending. The whales, flush from their performance, agreed to do it again. And so I got to see my son in the performance of his young life.

Lest you think that lightning doesn't strike twice, not long before Casey's last play, I became sick as a dog—and not with the nice little I-have-a-case-of-the-sniffles sick. No, I had the cannot-be-more-than-three-feet-away-from-the-bathroom type of sick.

Naturally, Buff was out of town (though, to be fair, had he been home, I'm not sure how much help he would have been). I'd already called in sick to work, but there was one little problem: the school play. *Casey's* school play.

Well, Casey had been asking me for weeks if I could get to her play, and I'd received special permission to leave the show early so I could beat feet to their school. Now that was no longer going to be necessary, since I was ensconced in the bathroom. The problem was pulling myself together enough to get to the school.

I managed to do it, though I sported the look my daughter and her friends refer to as "a hot mess." I yanked on a pair of velour pants, a cami with a cardigan pulled over the top, a newsboy cap to hide the mess that was my hair, and a ratty old ski jacket. Don't even ask if I wore makeup. I'm pretty sure you know the answer.

I toddled into the auditorium, where my girlfriends Stacy and Samantha were saving me a seat. (Even though they arrived nearly two hours early, the closest seats they could find were eight rows back.) I could feel the eyes of the Dreaded Super-Moms boring into the back of my head, and I wondered, *Is it because I'm the only one not carrying a Starbucks cup?*

I settled in nonetheless, struggling to sit up straight while battling waves of nausea, praying I wouldn't puke all over the Dreaded Super-Moms' hand-embroidered pony-skin boots. Mercifully, the nausea disappeared (well, almost) when the red velvet curtain rose. I anxiously scanned the stage, and then I found her. My Casey. The most beautiful brown bear I'd ever seen.

And you know what? She saw me, too. Even with all those

other parents and all those other sets of eyes, she saw me and visibly relaxed. Then she sang her heart out about the bear in the honey pit. I wasn't really paying attention.

She saw me, and that's all that mattered.

Eyes brimming with tears of happiness, I took out my camera to immortalize the tender moment.

The battery was dead.

playdates, or we don't rip eyes off teddy bears at our house

THERE HAVE BEEN MANY MARVELOUS IMPROVE-ments to society since the iPod-free dark ages when I was growing up. You know, things like e-mail communication so your husband can tell you the nanny is late when you're about to go live across America, portable DVD players so squirmy kids on long trips ask "Are we there yet?" only 56 times instead of 156 times, cell phones so you can be interrupted at work by aforementioned husband when he didn't get an immediate response back to his urgent e-mail, GPS for the map-impaired driver in the car who still will manage to get lost, TiVo and its handy-dandy remote control that I'll never be able to figure out in my lifetime, all that kind of stuff.

Why, I remember the thrill when I first got an electric typewriter. I took Casey and Cole in with me to Staples the other day and they saw a real, live typewriter, sitting dusty and forlorn on the shelf, and they asked me what it was.

"It's a *typewriter,*" I said, feeling older than Methuselah. "Before we had computers, you'd have to stick a piece of paper in and type right on it."

The look on their faces? Priceless.

And then I picked up a small bottle of opaque white liquid. "See this?" I went on. "When I used to type and I made a mistake, I'd have to use this stuff to cover over the mistake. You put it on with a little brush, and you had to wait for it to dry. Used to drive me crazy."

The look on their faces? I'd tell you, but they'd already moved on, over to the next aisle in search of something marginally more interesting. Anything to get away from one of Mommy's reminiscences about life in the dark ages.

So okay, having a computer keyboard to replace my hunt-and-peck routine at the typewriter is a massive improvement in my kids' lives. But I've got to say that there are a few things that can't compare. Back in the dark ages, when I got home from school, I didn't have five hours of homework and dance classes and karate and soccer and piano lessons and all the rest of those overscheduled headaches to think about.

I went out to play.

Yep, I went out to play with no supervision. And—Shock! Horror!—without a helmet, elbow guards, or knee pads. On playgrounds where the ground wasn't covered in bouncy rubber but in cold, hard concrete, and where the teeter-totters were designed to cause splinters if you were lucky enough not to fall off and crack your head open. I'd run down the street to my friends' houses, where the doors were never locked during the day, and we'd figure out what to do and where to play before running back outside.

Even if my mother could have called me on a cell phone, she wouldn't have needed to. I knew that I had to show up at home by dinnertime or I'd get clobbered.

So, when I was a kid, there was no such thing as a play-date. Wite-Out, yes. Scheduled-to-the-nanosecond organized "fun"—no way!

Now you just have to say the word "playdate," and plenty of moms like me break into a cold sweat. It's exhausting. Far few neighborhoods today feature streets where kids can just run wild and free, in and out of one another's houses, without schedules or supervision. So, managing the logistics of the playdate can be hell, especially if you have more than one child. Mommy has to have her finger on everybody else's plans for the day, or else everything will collapse in a hurry.

Setting up what should be a simple meeting invariably becomes complicated. When my son calls someone for a play-date, first he has to talk to his little buddy. Then you have to get on the phone with the other parent and negotiate what the kids said, and hopefully not contradict it, since we are totally out of the loop. Is he going to your house or coming to mine? What time is the pickup? Should we feed him dinner? How much is too much? Casey had her friend Kelsey coming over, and then Kelsey's mom was going to pick both of them up and Casey was going to spend the night at Kelsey's house, so Casey had to have all her stuff packed up, while Cole was going to Henry's house and he had to be picked up by a cer-tain time because Henry's mom had to go pick up his sister from *her* playdate, blah, blah, blah.

You can see how easy it becomes for playdates to spiral out of control.

Silly me thought the playdate situation would get better as the kids grew older. But it started to get worse in a hurry. *Much* worse. Oh, sure, I certainly knew that as school pressures and friendships deepened over time, it would be important for kids to know that they'd be able to see their friends regularly, after school hours, but organizing afternoons crammed with playdates on top of activities got to be a bit much.

One fine day I casually called one mom to schedule something, and she said, "Let me check his schedule."

Huh? *Schedule?* For an eight-year-old? I don't think an eight-year-old should have a schedule. Can't an eight-year-old just come home and relax?

That's it, I decided. From that day forward, there was a new rule about playdates, and it has made the setup of playdates a far more manageable hell.

The rule is simple: When school is in session, no more than two playdates, per kid, per week. Excluding weekends.

I can't believe I didn't think of this sooner, and some of my friends who've thanked me for the idea have said the same thing. Setting such a simple limit has helped Casey and Cole understand how to balance homework time, playdate time, and all-around decompressing time, and it's made for much more pleasant afternoons.

We also have another firm rule about what to do during playdates at our house: STAY OUTSIDE.

In the summer, when the weather is nice, the playdate rule is that I really don't want to see you in the house unless you're running in to use the bathroom, or you need a snack. See that big swing set we got from Costco? That is what that is for. It's for you, not for me. See the pool? That's for swimming. (As long as I can be nearby to supervise.) So get out there and play.

If the kids hem and haw, I'll hand them a ball and say, "Here. Take this orb and go outside and throw it around. See you later."

Or, if I'm in the mood—which I often am—I'll haul myself outside and join in the fun. It's play for the kids and hard-core aerobic exercise for me. When I bought Casey and Cole their own pogo sticks, I made sure to get one for me. I'll jump in the pool with them, and I'll run with them, and I'll chase Olivia and whatever's in her mouth with them.

In the winter, when it's freezing cold, I'll make sure the kids and their friends are bundled up, then tell them to go frolic in the snow. You need hot chocolate, fine, come to the door, have a nice hot sip, then STAY OUTSIDE.

Of course, winter playdates are always tough because the kids are in and out and they drop their backpacks, sodden boots, jackets, mittens, hats, and dripping snow pants all over the floor. Then they run upstairs to play, get bored, run back downstairs ten minutes later, slop on all their gear, race outside, and twenty minutes later the whole cycle starts over again.

Rules are crucial for the management of playdates. The unspoken rule—learned quickly by parents on playgrounds, where other kids are often running wild and misbehaving—is that you don't discipline other people's kids. Unless, of course, the offense is flagrant and someone gets hurt or something gets broken. I'm always on the lookout for the flagrant offenses, which happen when kids play, so if I catch someone biting, scratching, kicking, punching, or being sassy to someone else, that does not fly in our house. This kind of nag-o-matic behavior peaks in the toddler years, where the only words you'll hear with any regularity during playdates are "Mine!" "No, mine!" "No, mine!"

One smart mom I know minimized the "Mine!" "No, mine!" chorus by buying exact duplicates of preferred toys. Cheap little toys, naturally, like cars or small dolls. That usually prevented the "His is blue and mine is green and I hate green and I want blue and I want blue RIGHT NOW" whine that would surface precisely forty-two seconds after the moms beamed with pride at their kids while murmuring, "Isn't it lovely how *nicely* they share and play together?"

It's also tough for parents when their kid has a friend whose personality is as charming as chalk dragging across a blackboard. I'm pretty lucky that Casey and Cole like nice kids with nice parents, and on the odd occasion when they don't, I suppose I can tolerate any kid for a couple of hours. But where it gets tricky is when your kids have friends who act out in ways that bring out the worst in your formerly cuss-free child. You certainly don't want to choose your kids' friends for them, and of course you also know that the minute you say "You can't play with Herman," all your kid wants to do is have his new best friend Herman over all the time. You have to stay neutral. My tactic is to gradually call this kid less often, and call other kids more. Hopefully the situation will blow over, since kids can be fickle when it comes to friends, and they will usually move on to the next.

Or kids can be devoted to the point of dementia, as I was in the sixth grade. The object of my masochistic affection was one "Wendy." Well, Wendy ran so hot and cold I didn't know how she'd treat me from one minute to the next. She'd invite us all to her house and then ice someone out. It was just nasty. I can remember it as though it were yesterday!

But having survived Wendy and her Mean-Girl demeanor helps me now, while I watch my own daughter navigate her friendships during her playdates. I've seen her realize, painfully, that the people you love can still cause heartbreak in a friendship.

And as I've said already, you can't keep your kids from disappointment—in life, in love, with friends, in school, whatever. That's one of the reasons why I tend to talk with my kids about situations that happen at work or in my life—not to dump on them, but to make them aware that grown-ups have the same kinds of problems to solve. Casey, with her tender heart and innate sensitivity, particularly needs to hear this. Sometimes she finds it difficult to believe that when her friend is naughty, it's her friend's problem, not hers, and as such is no reflection on Casey.

I also spend plenty of time telling my kids about my own ups and downs with my friends, regaling them with stories of who I liked and who I didn't when I was a child, and especially about the time I got into a huge fight with my best friend because she told me I was no longer her best friend. Using my own ups and downs entertains Casey and Cole and can also lead to Teachable Moments. When I use concrete examples drawing upon my own experiences, I'm illustrating how friendships are fluid things, and how disagreements and misunderstandings can be long or short, or somewhere in between. Friends and circumstances and shared interests can shift and change over time. Friends make the world go round, but they aren't necessarily forever. Because I've had to move away from beloved friends (before e-mail!) as my career took me to new jobs around the country, I know how hard it is to not have familiar shoulders to cry on, and I know that building new friendships takes time, energy, and dedication. Leaving friends physically doesn't mean you leave them out of your heart.

Most of all, Casey and Cole learn that sometimes friends and the people you love make mistakes. They can make each other upset and angry and hurt—but if you really love someone and they love you, they're going to be there for you no matter what. If they aren't there, or if they're unwilling to deal with the situation that has caused pain, they're not your friends. Mourn their loss, and move on to a friend who'll treat you with more respect and love.

And if they have the PlayStation 3, even better.

mommy needs a playdate

GOOD FRIENDS ARE LIKE A COMFORTABLE BRA.
Every woman needs the right-size bra, with comfortable fabric that doesn't pinch or chafe or rub the wrong way, one that covers up your flaws and lifts and supports you where you need it the most.

Yep, my friends are just like my bras! Because behind every good-enough mother is another good-enough mother with whom to commiserate, shop, or just hang out and have a crab-fest. It's a healthy dose of friendship that fuels us to fight another day.

I can't imagine life without my friends. When I went to college, I waited tables at T.G.I. Friday's to pay my way, and it was no picnic. It was stressful and exhausting and I didn't have a lot of backup. One of the first lessons I learned was that when I felt myself getting behind on serving my tables, I had to tell people I needed help. Back then my fellow waitresses called this "being in the weeds." Let yourself get caught in the weeds, and you may very well get lost. Or drown.

Because I had to take care of myself from an early age, it's a little too easy for me to click into only-I-can-do-it mode from time to time. I'm a good-enough mother, right? I know I'm not perfect—nor do I strive for perfection either—but I should be able to cope with any challenge, right?

Well, the fact is that there's no need to go through mother-hood all by yourself.

That's what friends are for. Moms need playdates as much as their kids do. Friends are there to share the Omigod stories, to empathize with what unruly office mates can do, to tsk-tsk when the garage tries to overcharge you to fix the trans-mission, to laugh and scream and gossip about who's on the cover of the latest tabloid. They give you their own perspec-tive on how to deal with crabby husbands or partners, and strategies for dealing with issues with the kids at school. They're ideal to bounce ideas off of because they know what makes you tick.

Plus, they're a whole lot cheaper than a shrink!

There's no way to be a good-enough mother if you're not good enough to yourself. Coping with life's challenges takes energy. And friends are there to recharge the batteries when you feel you're running on empty.

Nothing fills up my depleted reserves more quickly than knowing I won't be judged by my friends. Our lives are hard enough without cluttering them up with people we don't even know well who pass judgment on us anyway. In fact, the very best of friends will love you unconditionally, for all the things that make you, you—including your perfectly imperfect par-enting. Like the time I called one friend and told her I was on my way to her house to pick up Casey, and she didn't know what I was talking about. Because Casey was at someone else's house, and I was so out of it I couldn't even remember where my own child was.

Friends are also invaluable reminders that while you might be a mom, you're still an adult with adult interests and needs. They know that in order to be the best good-enough mother you can be, you need to cultivate the whole person, away from your kids and husband. They can drag you away from the constant demands of your kids, and know that if your son screams "I hate you!" when you're on the way out the door to meet them, he'll just have to get over it.

Most of all, friends will say "Yes, your butt *does* look big in that dress" if, indeed, it really does.

And you'll have to admit they're right, because their advice and opinions are couched in love.

My very best girlfriend and soul mate is Stacy. We met in our town, Picketfenceville, when I was signing Casey and Cole up for after-school enrichment, activities that keep them at school and busy during the winter months when it's too cold for me to kick them outside to play. Well, I was signing Casey up, and Stacy happened to be the woman in charge of the paperwork, and she told me that her younger daughter, Kelsey, wanted a playdate with Casey. I said okay, and after that, a great friendship was born.

Stacy and I are so much alike. Like me, Stacy is a very busy woman with a full-time job in the media, running her own public relations company. I always joke that she and I exhibit the "two mommies/one brain" dynamic. Because our kids go to the same school, she and I have saved each other from the Mommy Who Messed Up Again award more times than I care to remember. I think that's why we gravitated toward each other. It was like, *Oh, good—here's someone else who's barely holding it together!* We give each other validation, especially because it helps to realize that we aren't crazy and we aren't the only ones who feel that we're barely keeping up on the treadmill that is life.

Plus, Stacy subscribes to the same good-enough mother philosophy. She knows all the mantras, especially my favorite, I Don't Care, and has no trouble following them either. She knows what's worth worrying about and what's got to wash off in the shower.

Which is why we're on the phone or e-mailing each other all the time, particularly when something noteworthy or cringe-worthy or just plain stupid happens. No matter what's gone down, we always manage to make each other feel better.

Stacy and I found a local Italian restaurant with owners savvy in the ways of parents who need a break. They set up one room as a sort of miniature Chuck E. Cheese, with arcade games and noise and flashing lights and tickets that can be redeemed for the kind of valuable prizes you know are going to either break or get lost in about thirty seconds. Best of all, it has a "party room" in the back, which, even though it's meant for birthday parties, is where Stacy and I have our own private parties. It's usually pretty empty, since the other parents prefer to supervise the screaming in the game room, and Stacy and I often sit there and happily yak over a glass of wine while our kids piss away seventy dollars' worth of tokens as they run from one activity to another.

Okay, maybe that's a slight exaggeration, but it's some ungodly number of tokens—and they are worth every penny, because we don't hear from the kids again until their pizza is there. Then they'll sit still for the two minutes it takes to scarf down a piece or two, and off they trot again. Stacy and I have solved all the problems of the world in the party room over a bottle of cheap white wine. Sure, we could have shared a fantastic meal somewhere in Manhattan for the same price (or less), but instead we inhale our kids' pizza crust and salad, and that's good enough for us. Actually, it's better than good enough—it's the *best*.

So I consider myself very fortunate to have such amazingly supportive bras—I mean friends. Without them, I don't know how well I'd manage the chaos. With them, I manage to scrape along, safe in the knowledge that they're my invisible safety net, always there, ready to catch me if I fall.

mothering my mother

ONE DAY WHEN COLE WAS EIGHT AND BEING his usual charming self, I told him, "Hey, man, don't try pulling the wool over my eyes. I've been eight years old before and I know what it's like."

That worked for, oh, maybe a minute, and then it was back to more of the same. So I ended up saying the one thing to Cole that my mother used to always say that drove my sister and me crazy: "I do so much for you guys, the least you could do is . . ."

Omigod, *I'm turning into my mother!*

I suspect that nearly all moms think this from time to time. Okay, I bet that 100 percent of all moms *know* this is true. So much of the way we parent is learned from our own mothers—the good and the bad.

The good is that my mom's such an interesting character, part Iroquois Indian, beautiful and creative and independent. She'd never hesitate to get down on the floor and play cards with my sister and me. I always knew how much she loved me with a fierce, unconditional love. She believed in me and encouraged me to strive for the best I could be, and comforted me when I had a hard time being the school wallflower and late bloomer.

The bad was that toward the end of their marriage, Mom and Dad fought in front of us. A lot.

To be fair, of course, my mom had her hands full with me and my sassiness. When I was twelve and those hormones were starting to kick in, I decided that I was going to stay a tomboy since all things girly really got on my nerves. I loudly declared that I hated my first name, Michelle, and that I was going to change it to Mike. Well, Mom took all the helium out of my balloon when she told me to go right ahead, since her own deep, dark secret was that her real name was Florence (and yes, she will KILL me for putting that in print), and she never liked it so she used Anne instead. Crushed, I went with my middle name, René, as an alternative—because I certainly wasn't going to stick with Mike if Mom gave it her blessing!

After the Mike incident, though, I don't think Mom ever quite figured out the force that she was up against.

Compounding my orneriness was the undeniable fact that my parents stayed married for twenty-four years, probably about four too many. When my mom ultimately decided that her marriage could no longer survive, my parents separated, and Dad moved out. Mom had to move to Southern California to revive her career in her midforties as a military reserve recruiter, and Tracy and I stayed put so we could finish our schooling.

Suddenly we were parentless. I was eighteen and Tracy was sixteen. I had started college, yet was weighted with the responsibilities of taking charge of my sister and managing the house. Trust me, I didn't *want* to be in charge.

Fortunately for both of us, Tracy soon went to stay with

Mom. Unfortunately for both of us, Dad soon became very, very sick.

Actually, he hadn't been well for a long time. He'd already survived breast cancer, as one of the roughly fifteen hundred cases diagnosed in men each year. I remember very little about it, because I was only about twelve when he was diagnosed. I do remember that I was young enough to still be embarrassed by the word "breast."

For reasons unknown to me now, my father chose to have a radical mastectomy. Again, I remember little about the operation, but a lot more about his recovery. He had a horrific scar that stretched from under his armpit to his sternum. It made him look concave and lopsided.

I also remember my mother chiding him to do the exercises the doctor prescribed so he wouldn't have a limited range of motion on that side. Dad, as stubborn as he was, didn't do the exercises, and he could lift his arm only as high as his shoulder for the remainder of his life.

But there still are several things I do remember quite vividly about my dad. He was an excellent provider, but he suffered from high blood pressure, diabetes, and heart disease. He recuperated from a mild stroke. By the time I was a teen, breast cancer was just another item to add to his long list of ailments.

Right before he died, Dad went to the hospital because he needed to change his medication, and it couldn't be done on an outpatient basis. While there, he took a turn for the worse, and the doctor told me that I had better call whatever family I had to be with him because it wasn't looking good.

I grabbed the phone to call Mom, and she was still so

angry at him about everything that had gone wrong between them that she said she wasn't going to come see him. My blood started to boil. There I was at twenty-three, already stressed to the max with full-time studies and my exhausting job as a waitress, barely managing to make ends meet, with Dad nearing the end. So I told Mom in no uncertain terms that she *had* to come up to Sacramento and say good-bye.

She grudgingly came up with my sister and spent some time with Dad. Later that night he had a massive stoke, and he died a few weeks later. He was only fifty-nine.

Along with the grief I felt for the loss of my father, I also mourned the loss of innocence I'd had to endure because I'd had to so painfully mother my mother.

As any mother of a daughter knows, the mother-daughter relationship is incredibly complex. I believe it is also much more difficult to manage than a mother-son relationship. I love my mom to death, but there's a weird sort of dichotomy because she's never been one to embrace the changing of our relationship. To her I will always be her little-bitty girl. This was kind of hard to take when I was parenting my sister as a teen myself, or having to beg my mom to come as my dad lay dying. Back then this little-bitty girl was plenty dang pissed at her mom for acting like a little-bitty girl herself.

As I graduated from college and threw myself whole-heartedly into moving forward in my career, our relationship finally made a calm, natural progression. I didn't love my mom any less, but I *needed* her less. I was working, I could take care of my own bills (once I took them out of the shoe box in the closet and actually paid them), and basically I grew up and became fully self-actualized. At this point Mom *tried* to treat me like a grown-up—sort of. She didn't succeed, but I was able to let it go, and since we didn't spend huge chunks of time together, or live in the same city, we developed a smoother and less-charged bond.

When Casey was born, the first thing my mother said was, "This child is *not* calling me Grandma." In her mind Grandma was someone who sat in a rocking chair with a scowl on her face and her hair coiled in a little gray bun.

"My name is *Meema*," Mom declared.

In 1997, when I was three months pregnant with my son, I was in a blissful state of mind. My life was progressing swimmingly. I was the *perfect* mom to my daughter and the *perfect* daughter to my mom. (Note sarcasm.)

Then came the call.

It was late December and Mom was on the phone, sounding calm and unruffled even as she asked if I was sitting down. I told her I was. Then she dropped a lightning bolt from out of the blue. She'd been diagnosed with breast cancer.

Through my shock I asked myself, *How could that be?* Anne Syler, who was sixty-five at the time, and who had always been healthy, who ate a well-balanced diet before nutritionists chided us all to do the same (don't get me started on her penchant for aloe vera juice), and who exercised regularly before it was all the rage, had been diagnosed with breast cancer. But, unfortunately, breast cancer can strike anyone, and my mom had become just another one of the more than two hundred thousand women who are diagnosed with breast cancer each year in the United States.

Once again, breast cancer became an unwelcome member of my family.

Mom went on to tell me that it was a good news/bad news type of situation. The bad news was the breast cancer diagnosis. The good news was that it was caught very early, thanks to her regularly scheduled mammogram and an eagle-eyed radiologist. So it was a tiny stage-zero breast cancer. Frankly, if you're going to get cancer, this is the kind you want to get. Cancers at this stage are less than a centimeter in diameter, and the survival rate for stage-zero breast cancer is almost 100 percent.

I didn't know that yet. My mind was reeling. The thing about a cancer diagnosis is that once you hear about the Big C, many times you don't hear anything else.

You are convinced that the Big C equals the Big D.

Death.

Which, thank goodness, is something I now know to be *not* true—with one notable caveat: The Big C must be detected early, as it had been with my mom. She could be the poster child for early detection and the vital importance of a regular, yearly mammogram.

After meeting with her doctors and doing a bit of her own research, Mom told me she was going to go for the lumpectomy, followed by six weeks of radiation. No way was I going to permit her to make this decision entirely on her own, so I insisted that I wanted to speak to her doctor and help her figure out what to do.

Off we went on this journey for which we had no road map—just feeling around in the dark. I became the wingman (wingwoman?) in my mom's dogfight. I'm what the Susan G. Komen Breast Cancer Foundation people call a co-survivor. For me the journey was fraught with anxiety, as I, the *perfect*

René Syler

daughter, was living and working in Dallas at the time, and Mom lived in San Antonio. So I immediately hauled my bloated carcass onto a plane to San Antonio, to be with her and to meet her doctor. It was then that I removed the crown of *perfection* and put on the news-gathering hat. And with my pen and paper in hand, I began to quiz the oncologist about my mom's cancer and her treatment options.

First we heard about the stages of breast cancer more advanced than my mom's: Stage-one breast cancer has a 95 percent five-year survival rate. Chances are extremely high that you're going to be all right.

Stage-two breast cancer shows a pretty big drop. The five-year survival rate is about 85 percent.

Stage-three breast cancer has some pretty grim statistics. The five-year survival rate is only about 50 percent—if you get the best possible care. It's almost always 100 percent fatal within five years without the most aggressive, progressive, and determined care.

Stage-four breast cancer has a 20 percent cure rate, so chances are slim that you will survive it.

I said a fervent thank-you prayer that Mom was still at stage zero and had two options: breast-conserving lumpectomy with radiation, or a mastectomy. Well, Mom was a young sixty-five at the time, attached to her breasts and they to her. She chose the lumpectomy. Along with that, she would need six weeks of radiation therapy, which she was less than enthusiastic about.

What threw her about the radiation was remembering her own mother's valiant but ultimately losing battle with lymphoma, and the radiation she'd had to endure. So Mom had this totally understandable fear of what radiation entailed, and she dragged her feet and vacillated. Maybe she would go through with it, maybe she wouldn't.

She was driving me crazy. I had several stern talks with her. The perfect daughter, newswoman par excellence, had now become . . . this! The nag-o-matic!

Oh yeah, I also had to bring out my pitchfork and tell her, "Yes, you *will* do what your doctor recommends—and you will do it *now*! Your doctor said you need the radiation; let's trust her and get going."

As this drama—which to my mind was wholly unnecessary—unfolded, I became more and more upset. Not just because my mom was digging in her heels, but because I was a pregnant mom who was actually in need of some mothering myself.

So instead of remaining calm and collected, when my mother would start her I'm-not-gonna-radiate routine, I'd fly off the handle, thinking, *Why are you doing this? Don't hate me for loving you so much!*

And then I'd tell her, "You listen to me. You're going to do everything that doctor says you're going to do, within reason. The doctor's not on crack. The doctor knows what she's talking about. And if she says you're going to go out there and eat a bale of hay every day, you better start munching now!"

I'd stop, take a deep breath, and screech, "Don't forget that you *will* have a positive attitude, because, as we know, that is integral to the outcome! And you will survive!"

I think she agreed to the radiation just to shut me up.

Mom had her surgery on a Thursday morning. I couldn't be there for her because I had to go back to work. I was racked with guilt, but you know what? In that time, the perfect daughter and newswoman par excellence had donned another hat.

Nurse! I made it down from Dallas several times during her recovery. And during that time, she talked; I listened. She cried. I hugged her. And through it all we celebrated. We gave thanks that she had caught her cancer so early.

We also gave thanks that she had good insurance and didn't have the additional worry about whether or not she'd be struggling to pay her medical bills.

And most of all we gave thanks for her *perfect* daughter.

Okay, so I'm sticking that in to make sure you're still with me!

Fast-forward nearly nine years. . . . I mark my mother's years of being cancer-free by looking at my son and remembering the tiny baby I was carrying when she was diagnosed. I no longer jump when I hear her voice on the phone, as she now e-mails me the news after her yearly mammogram. Usually her e-mails are some tired jokes that have been around the Internet since it was first invented, or other downloads that mess up my computer, but her no-cancer-now e-mails are always welcome.

Good-enough mother that I am, I'd like to think that I had a hand in my mother's survival (although, to be blunt, I probably didn't!). And just like me, I'm sure there are many of you who've had to don the devil's horns to prompt loved ones into doing what they needed to do. For me, at least, I only did what came naturally, the only thing I really knew how to do. And when I joined other volunteers at the Susan G. Komen Breast Cancer Foundation, I found kindred spirits who felt and acted exactly as I had—who totally understood what being a nag-o-matic meant!

Although my mom has mercifully been cancer-free for these nine years, I'm still in mothering-my-mother mode, and have accepted the fact that I will be till she passes on (which hopefully won't be for a very long time).

But it's really hard to be thrust into a role—any kind of role—when you haven't asked for it. I think it's a fair guess that most of the parents reading this book made a deliberate choice to become a parent. How many of us made a deliberate choice to mother our mothers?

I couldn't help thinking about this when my mom was diagnosed, and I realized that I was one of the few people in this country whose parents have both had breast cancer. It suddenly dawned on me that breast cancer would always be a part of my life.

Then it was my turn.

In September 2004, I went for my regular, routine mammogram, which I've been doing every year since my mother was diagnosed. This time the results were anything but regular and routine. Instead, I was thrust into a world that, until that point, I had only observed and reported on. After my first biopsy, I was diagnosed with a condition called hyperplasia with atypia, or a pre-pre-cancer. With this condition, cells are growing rapidly and dividing in a suspicious manner, but it's not yet cancer.

When I heard that, I heaved a sigh of relief. Until my doctor told me how close I had come to being diagnosed with cancer that day. (In fact, he told me he'd been almost certain it was cancer, thank you very much!) After my treatment—which consisted of nothing more difficult than watchful waiting—he told me bluntly that this condition raises a woman's chances, by up to five times, of developing breast cancer sometime in the near future. In fact, he was almost certain he was going to diagnose me with breast cancer at some point in my life, sooner rather than later.

As you can imagine, I was not exactly thrilled with this information. But it could have been much worse, of course. For now, the hyperplasia diagnosis means that I have to be closely monitored with regular mammograms, self-checks, doctor visits, and other tests for the rest of my life.

Statistics vary a bit, but between 1 and 5 percent of breast cancers have a genetic link. Since both of my parents had breast cancer, my doctors are very concerned, especially as male breast cancer tends to have a genetic component. In fact, they were worried enough about me to urge genetic testing to see whether or not I carry the breast cancer gene.

Even I, the take-charge get-your-radiation-now-Mom-or-else perfect daughter, was resistant to the idea of any testing for a long time, until I thought about my children. Who would do my daughter's hair or kiss my son's scraped knee if I weren't here? I refuse to let them grow up without their mommy. I also thought about the breast cancer figures. Of those more than two hundred thousand women diagnosed with breast cancer each year, forty thousand die as a result. And I knew it was important for me to have the test done so that I could be more informed and prepared.

So I bit the bullet and recently underwent genetic testing to see if I had the specific gene that is a marker for breast cancer. It involved a simple blood draw (and, unfortunately, a whopping payment of three thousand dollars not covered by insurance). It turns out that I do not have either gene linked to breast cancer.

I can remember, years ago, when I first began working with the Susan G. Komen Breast Cancer Foundation, that I really wanted a platform from which to spread the word about breast cancer and early detection. Little did I know it would happen for me on national television. I decided to chronicle my experience of hyperplasia with atypia for viewers of *The Early Show*. After all, even with the Internet, television remains a powerful medium with a vast reach to people all over America. It was my hope that if viewers saw a relatively young woman in good health, who eats right, exercises, and doesn't drink too much, go through a breast cancer scare, then they would realize it could happen to anyone.

Another reason was more selfish.

As much as I like to talk, it was, quite frankly, difficult to open up to others about my own experience and to express my fears. Sure, I had had no trouble talking to the other Komen volunteers—many of whom have become friends—about my parents' cancers, but it was difficult for me to talk about my own situation. So it was paradoxically very cathartic for me to use the camera to tell my story, even though I had no idea, at first, whether or not the segment would strike a chord with viewers.

I can't begin to express how astonished and humbled I was by the response. Our Web site got twenty thousand hits in a week. I received countless e-mails, cards, and letters from people who said I made them late to work because they couldn't leave without finding out how my story ended. People who said they cried when I cried. I was particularly touched by the number of people who said they prayed for me. And I was thrilled by the many women who told me they'd scheduled mammograms because I got over my fears and shared my story with the millions of women who needed to hear it. Mammograms help detect breast cancer tumors before they can get bigger, I told them. Early detection and vigilance are that simple. I know my mom is still here today because of the mammogram that saved her life.

My case, however, is not so rosy. I already get regular mammograms and MRIs, and do monthly self-exams. A scant six months ago I had to have a deep needle biopsy when my doctor spotted some calcifications that were weirder than usual. This was an incredibly painful procedure, and I was a wreck waiting for the biopsy results—which, thank God, were negative.

And for as much grief as I sometimes give her, I do feel that my mother is the only one who truly understands what I go through whenever I have my mammograms and biopsies. She is the only one who, instead of offering empty assurances, breathes a deep sigh each time and utters two simple words: "I know."

There's something "I know" too. I sure am lucky to have Anne Syler as my mom.

Until someone calls her Grandma.

the boys vs. girls clothing smackdown

THERE ARE NO DESIGNER LABELS IN OUR HOUSE. *YET.*

A healthy self-image isn't just predicated on the clothes we wear. Being conscious of body image, and especially how our world has misguidedly placed a high value on women's bodies starved to the point of anorexia (and men's bodies that are hair-free and rippled with six-packs), is an issue all moms need to discuss with their children.

Although I was a longtime resident of Geekville as a child, I now have the confidence to feel comfortable in my own skin—and what I put on it. Sometimes I'd get asked what Buff thought about the outfit I wore on *The Early Show* that morning. In an instant, I was out with the answer: "It doesn't matter what Buff thinks about what I'm wearing—*it's what René thinks about what René is wearing that counts!*"

You know where that confidence comes from? My early years in television.

One time, many, many years ago, when I was first starting in TV, Mark Mayhew, one of the best news directors I'd ever worked for, pulled me aside.

"Listen, René," he told me, "you're going to have a lot of

people who will like you, a lot who will not like you, and a lot who not only will not like you but who will also have suggestions on how to change you. If you listen to every one of those people, you're going to lose the essence of *you*.

"If one person says to you, 'I don't like your hair,' so you change your hair color, and then another says, 'You need to change your makeup,' and another says, 'You need to change your clothes,' there will be precious little of the new you that resembles the old you. You may as well stick with what you've got and risk these people not liking it, instead of selling out."

Over the years I've said many prayers of gratitude to Mark for giving me such great advice. I often think of it when my kids are watching TV or leafing through the copious piles of magazines I bring home to go through for work, seeing one superskinny girl or model or actress after another. I'll take the opportunity to say something like, "Wow, can you believe how thin that girl is? She's *way* too thin. See her bones sticking out? See her holding a dirty martini and sucking on a butt? This is *not* normal. *Mommy* is normal."

They roll their eyes, and I brace myself for the day that's coming very soon—the day when my daughter succumbs to the Attack of the Killer Wannabes and starts pleading for the same hundred-dollar jeans she sees on the other girls at school.

Oh, sure, there are those mothers (usually of the Dreaded Super-Mom variety) who are mad for clothes and schedule their vacations around designer trunk shows, and whose children are always spotlessly dressed in fashion so forward it hasn't even been marked down yet. That ain't me. My kids won't be sporting hand-knit cashmere (what, you mean I can't throw it in the washer?) or Italian leather Mary Janes more expensive than caviar (Olivia will shred them as part of her favorite meal before you can say "Bah!") or buttery suede jackets that'll be irreparably stained and torn as soon as Cole forgets his on the bus (Besides, suede just happens to be Olivia's *second* favorite meal!).

There are three reasons why I'm never going to be into labels.

The first reason is that clothes do not a person make. I don't judge people on appearance and neither will my kids. I've mentioned already that Casey and Cole like to ask me and Buff if we're rich, and we always tell them that if having a nice house, warm clothes in the winter and cool clothes in the summer, parents who love you to death, and the opportunity to get a good education means we're rich, then yes, we're not just rich—we're loaded!

But if a ten-year-old needs to wear a mink shrug to feel rich, well, then I feel for the poor misguided kid, and sentence her parents to life in polyester prison.

The second reason is that I grew up equating shopping with a jaunt to one of Dante's circles of hell. Because my parents were both in the military, our family did most of our shopping on base. Sure, they had top-quality clothes—as long as you didn't mind that they were past their sell-by date. Jeans would cost $7.99, and they fit perfectly well, but they were plain as pie.

When I was in sixth grade, all the other girls had trendy jeans, which fit better than perfectly well and had that fancy-schmancy swirly script that read *Jordache* emblazoned on their perky little butts. So I wanted Jordache jeans too. Anne

Syler looked at me as if I had grown a third eye overnight and screeched, "What, are you totally insane, child? You must be out of your freaking mind if you think I'm going to pay $69.99 for a pair of jeans!"

Hence my beginnings as a bargain shopper, devoid of any designer jeans, and a bargain shopper I remain. I'd say that about three quarters of my wardrobe, on the air and at home, is stuff that I got on sale at either the outlet shops at Woodbury Common, or at my beloved T.J. Maxx, Filene's Basement, Loehmann's, Marshalls, Kohl's, or Target. I don't need mirrors that take off five pounds on the walls of plush dressing rooms, or fawning sales ladies in posh emporiums.

What I need is a discount!

I think those with a penchant for bargain shopping have usually spent years being broke, and have learned how to spend money efficiently in order to survive. I know I did. The one thing I have picked up from Mr. Checkbook-Balancer, my husband, is that just because you make money, it doesn't mean that you have to spend every dime. It's best to be fiscally prudent. You have to do grown-up things like set up savings accounts and retirement accounts. I'm determined to set a good example about budgets and value, and I do discuss with my children how much hard work it takes to earn money. I also make it clear to them that even though it may be hard to hear So-and-So brag about her designer togs, our money can be better spent on items of value, particularly those that won't be outgrown in a scant few months.

What I want to impress upon my kids is that while being clad in appropriate clothing is a necessity, spending a fortune on designer labels is *not*. Where clothing is concerned, what counts are function and looks, not labels. As long as you look good and feel good, what you're wearing is plenty good enough.

What I don't discuss with my kids, though, is the satisfyingly deep frisson of joy you can get when the jacket you've been eyeing has been slashed from a ridiculous eight hundred dollars to a far more manageable one fifty and you can save six hundred fifty dollars to either spend on something else or sock away for a rainy day. They'll be better able to appreciate this when they're older.

The third reason I'm not into designer labels is that, while I may love trawling through the racks at Target or T.J. Maxx for myself or for gifts for others, I'd rather have a root canal than go clothes shopping with my kids. Not because choosing the garments is a big deal; it isn't. But because kids with an attention span the length of a gnat's wing tend not to do well in the interminable checkout lines at my favorite discount outlets.

Last summer was the summer of sugar and TV and it was also the summer of too many late nights. In early August, I planned one weekend for us to hang out as a family and play on Saturday, and then the plan was for us to go on a family shopping excursion to the huge mall at Woodbury Common on Sunday for clothes and other essential items. Well, we had so much fun scarfing down microwave popcorn as we surveyed the vast, empty wasteland that is cable TV on a summer Saturday night that silly me let Casey and Cole stay up really late.

Silly, *silly* me!

Why, oh why, do I always think it's a great idea to let the

kids stay up late on weekends when I know the next day there will be hell to pay and I'll be first in line at the register?

By the time I roused the kids in the morning, I might as well have been dragging two aircraft carriers across dry land. One of my pet peeves when I hold hands with Casey and Cole is how they walk—dragging their feet—when they're tired. Which makes me hiss at them to pick up their feet and *move*. Which makes them complain about how pooped they are and how they want to go home. Nag, *nag*, whine, *whine*.

That miserable expedition was entirely my fault. Never take kids shopping, even to a toy store, when they're tired and cranky. It was an especially dumb move because I prefer to make the most of the shopping schlep with the kids by turning it into a learning experience whenever possible, but this time they were too tired to be interested. I normally get a real kick out of teaching my daughter the fine points of bargain-shopping, especially the art of cheap chic—you know, buying one really expensive piece and pairing it with something from Target. I do it all the time. Viewers of my shows were often treated to a $5.99 tank top under a Dolce & Gabbana jacket!

During our shopping expeditions I'll also tell Casey how important it is to choose and wear what you like, not what your friends like or say is a must-have, or what other people tell you looks good on you—what *you* like.

I'd already lost so many battles in the War of the Morning Dress that I'd surrendered years ago. From an early age Casey and Cole made clear their specific likes and dislikes about what they were going to wear, and that was fine with me. (Plus I also feel like part of good-enough mothering is fostering my children's individuality. If they like something that strikes me as hideous, I act like a side seam and zip it.) I finally wised up and abdicated total responsibility for their choices, so long as they weren't out running around in the snow in their bathing suits.

Even when she was a little girl, I'd buy Casey these cute little outfits from Target, and then watch in dismay as she toddled over to her closet, ignored them, and pulled out what she wanted to wear. There were yellow shorts and a yellow top that went together perfectly, but she wanted to wear the yellow shorts and green top.

Like, *duh*! It finally dawned on me that my kids were people, not projects, and they had a right to their opinions, whether about the color of a shirt or the pattern on a pair of pants. It wasn't the end of the world if their tastes weren't mine and they preferred clash to cute.

Besides, children are so powerless when it comes to most other choices in their lives. They can't choose their school or their teachers or the food you cook for them or the size of their house. Heck, they can't even choose their parents. Allowing them to have the final say about their clothing choices empowers them and shows them that you have confidence in their decisions and trust them to make decent ones (even if you don't like plaid mixed with flowers). It spares you the War of the Morning Dress and frees you up to concentrate on other, more important issues. And it sure saves a lot in clothing bills or time spent in the returns line when they've rejected whatever adorable item you were sure they were going to like.

So when a friend told me that his wife goes nuts because their eight-year-old son wants to wear only camouflage shirts and pants, I replied, "So what? Let him. I mean, what's wrong with camouflage for a kid of eight? It's not a reflection on you; it's what your kid likes. I'm really grateful my kids know what they want to wear."

We all have to choose the hill we're gonna die on, and so I'll keep my pistol holstered when it comes to clothes.

One friend told me she made a badge that read I DRESSED MYSELF TODAY and used to pin it on her daughter's rather unusual outfits. That worked like a charm for her. (Frankly, I don't think you even need a badge, as I think it's pretty obvious when a child pulls an outfit together!)

I've learned my lesson. So now when we shop together, I always ask my kids, "Do you like that? Are you going to wear it? Are you sure? I'm not buying you something you don't like, and if you change your mind later, I'm not buying you something else to replace it." Even the cheapest bargain becomes a total waste of money if your child hates it and refuses to put it on.

Cole went through a phase when all he wanted to wear were football jerseys with large numbers on them, so I high-tailed it to Wal-Mart and picked up a whole bunch—for only $9.99 each! Oh, lucky day!—along with some cargo pants. He wore them to bed, to school, to the doctor, you name it. He was happy, and my budget was happy that this phase lasted for more than a year. Until Olivia got her teeth into the latest batch and shredded them before I even had a chance to cut the tags off.

When this phase was going on, Buff would stubbornly buy all these great polo shirts for Cole—shirts that only Buff liked. After a few months of this, I told Buff to cut it out, because I knew Cole was *not* going to wear them. It was one of the few times when I was actually more savvy about our budget than my husband was, and let me tell you, I sure knew how to rub it in!

What is it with dads and polo shirts, anyway? My old colleague Harry Smith told me that when his kids were small, they never wanted to dress up. His youngest son hated to wear anything with a collar. All he wanted to wear were T-shirts.

And now that this boy is a teenager, what does he favor? Polo shirts.

Speaking of phases, there was the time when Cole was about two-and-a-half and obsessed with nail polish. Buff freaked out, but I told him to let it go. Allow Cole to paint his nails now and he'll grow out of it. Plus as he gets older, the peer pressure will (unfortunately) kick in. Cole needed to find this out on his own. And he did.

Except that a few weeks ago Cole did ask if he could put some nail polish on. I told him he could do mine instead.

"Fine," he said, "but I want to wear a mud mask instead."

Yep, Cole is the kind of boy who knows what he wants. He grew his hair out into dreads that were absolutely adorable. I just loved them. So when he told me he was sick of them and wanted to whack them off, my knee-jerk reaction was to tell him no, because they were so darn cute. But he protested that he wanted an Afro because all the basketball players have Afros.

When I thought about my knee-jerk reaction, however, I realized it wasn't just about how cute his dreads were, but about the difference between eight-year-old Cole and ten-year-old René. Cole has no problem stating what he wants; I did. When my dad took me for a haircut at a barbershop, the barber thought flat-chested little me was a boy, and gave me a boy's Afro cut, which was way up around the ears and high in the back. Believe it or not, I was too shy (yes, me!) to say anything as simple as "STOP! I'M A GIRL!"

So if Cole wants to cut his hair, let him cut his hair. I'll teach him how to take care of it.

As much as I'd hate it, it's what I want him to be—a child who can make his own decisions.

the birds and the bees

"GUESS WHAT, MOMMY! I'M JUST LIKE DAD!"
Cole announced as he flew into my office at home.

"What do you mean?" I asked, putting down my notes.

"Oh, you know," he said proudly. And then he showed me how he'd stuffed an extra pair of drawers inside his pants to, *ahem*, fill himself out.

This is the same boy who asked me the other day if I fed him when he was little. Of course I did, I told him. But what he really wanted to know was did I *breast-feed* him.

See, even at eight he's a breast man!

I don't know a whole lot of moms who find it easy to talk to their kids about sex and biology and how their private parts work. Do you remember the first time your little boy pointed to his testicles and asked, "Why are these things here? What do they do?" Or when your little girl asked you why her baby brother has "that thing down there" that she doesn't?

When I was in school, the word "sex" was a total taboo. Sexual behavior wasn't discussed, except in the biological reproduction sense. So rather than "sex education" we had "health" lectures when we were in sixth grade. The boys and girls were separated into two giggling groups, and we learned about what a period was, and God only knows what they told the boys, because the boys sure as heck never told us!

I don't think my health teacher did a particularly sterling job, as I clearly remember having the crap scared out of me, and then going home to tell my mother that I needed to start carrying tampons and pads because I could start my period at any minute. At that point I was a less than zero on the Tanner scale that measures development at puberty. Literally, there were boards with more bumps than I had. I still thought cramps were what you got when you ate too much chocolate.

Things will be different for Casey and Cole. Times have changed and now there's so much great information out there about sexual development, presenting the facts in a non-threatening and child-friendly way, that I can use these guides if my own instincts somehow fail me. I think that if you just present information about anything sexual as factual and normal, kids will simply satisfy their curiosity and move on. They won't get crazy or overtly curious if discussions are always presented calmly. Hem and haw and redden and get crazy about it as if there's something to hide, or to feel shameful about, and you might find your kid playing doctor when you thought he was playing Nintendo.

I should have heeded my own advice, back when the kids were small and we were having some fun with my step-daughter, Tracy.

"Do you remember when we were playing Scrabble with the kids—and drinking wine—and you spelled the word 'ho'?" she reminded me recently. "And you exclaimed, 'Hey—that's a word, isn't it?' And I just looked at you and then nodded toward the kids."

Oops.

"Gee, I don't know what I was thinking," I quickly said at the time. "'Ho' is not a word."

"Yes it is, Mommy," Casey said. "It's what Santa says. Ho, ho, ho!"

Tracy had to go into the bathroom, shut the door, and run the water for ten minutes so the kids wouldn't hear her laughing.

What I try to do is give Casey and Cole as much age-appropriate information as they need and then move on. You know how literal kids can be, especially when they've over-heard something that they don't quite yet understand, so you try to be as straightforward as you can be, answering only the questions asked. It's not as though you can have one "talk" and then consider the job done. The "talk" for my kids started when they were toddlers.

One time, when Cole was about three, we were out driving in our old neighborhood in Dallas and I saw a baby in a small swing hanging from a large branch of a tree in his yard, and I said, "Look at that baby in the tree, Cole."

"How did he get there?" Cole asked.

"I'm sure his mommy put him there," I replied.

"No, how did the baby get *here*?" he persisted.

Oh, brother, I thought, *here we go.* So I gave him the whole "there's a garden and a seed grows, and the seed is planted in the mommy's uterus and the baby grows" spiel. That was enough for him at three.

Then at five Cole became more particular.

"How does the seed *get* in there?" he wanted to know.

Oh, brother, I thought. *Where's Buff when I need him?* Never mind. I did my best. I didn't mind. Cole's eyes glazed over with boredom after a minute or two, and he ran out to play. *Mission accomplished,* I thought.

Well, a few nights later Casey was taking a bath, and Cole was sitting near me, playing with some of his toys.

"Mommy," he asked, "when is Casey's baby coming?"

"What do you mean?" I asked, perplexed.

"You know, the baby that's growing in her tummy."

Guess I hadn't accomplished the mission after all.

"There's no baby growing in her tummy right now."

"Why not?" he asked.

I went through my seed-is-planted spiel again, and this time Cole's eyes didn't glaze over. They lit up.

"Well, I know I'm going to have two kids," he announced.

"How do you know?" I asked.

"Because I have two seeds right here," he replied, pointing to his testicles.

Yep, if the seed spiel doesn't work, you might want to consider a small pet. My cowriter Karen's son, Emmanuel, marched into kindergarten and proudly announced, "My toads were mating last night!" and his teacher was especially thrilled to hear it.

Surprisingly, Cole hasn't asked me any more questions. So far. And when he does, I'll make sure that Buff does his utmost to improve upon my seed spiel.

I'm going to have to get it together, though, because when we went to Orlando on our annual Walt Disney World jaunt last year, I nearly had a meltdown. I was lounging by the pool at our hotel, when these girls came by who'd been in puberty for all of forty-seven minutes, and they were parading around with their tattoos and belly-button rings and teeny-tiny bikinis and flat tummies and attitude to match. They couldn't have been more than twelve or thirteen. I thought to myself, *You know what—that's a* bad *idea.*

Will Casey morph into a trash-talking hell-raiser with a double-D cup when she's their age, throwing a fit when I won't allow her to pierce her belly button, nose, and nipples? That can't possibly happen to my sweet little Casey, can it?

I don't think so. You know why? Because I'll show her my belly. Not that I have a tattoo or anything, but if I did, what once used to read "super" might as well now be "supercalifragilisticexpialidocious," after two kids—with stretch marks!

Casey had been watching those girls too, as she sat with her towel wrapped around her so no one could see her. Once again, I said a fervent prayer of thankfulness that she has an innate modesty about her. Whenever she sees me kissing or hugging Buff, he'll tease her by calling me his girlfriend, and Casey's reaction will be to roll her eyes, stick out her tongue, and regale us with an "Oh, *gross!*"

On the other hand, good-enough mothers don't sweat the small stuff, and there's no point in making yourself crazy about stuff that hasn't happened yet—as well as stuff that you have no control over. If Casey is going to get her period at eleven, she's going to get it—and there's nothing that I can do to stop it.

Casey *has* become intensely interested in the books American Girl puts out, explaining puberty and bras and deodorant and shaving and cramps and all that stuff that makes a young girl (and her mother) want to weep. I try to be very low key about the whole process. Whenever I catch her reading one of those books, I'll ask her mildly if there's anything she wants to talk about, and reassure her that if she ever has any questions, I'll be happy to answer them.

I like to tease the kids by saying that one reason I go to the gym is so Mommy can be the one with the best figure in the house, but I can tell Casey is going to far surpass me. She's going to be beautiful. She already *is* beautiful—she was a beautiful baby, she is a beautiful girl, and as a teenager she's going to be a knockout.

This isn't mommy pride speaking; it's the truth. And it's a source of immense pride and pleasure, coupled with a tremendous responsibility to help her deal with the price of beauty. She needs to be taught how to handle the unwanted attention she'll be sure to get, and she needs to be comfortable with herself and her body, starting now. I need to help her hone her instincts so she'll automatically know what's okay and what's not going to fly, so that she has the voice to speak up when she's uncomfortable.

Thankfully, she's still my little girl with a flat chest, but that doesn't mean we're not thinking about what's to come. When she got out of the shower the other day and told me, "Oh, I forgot to do my armpits," I blandly replied that she was probably fine.

"No, I'm not sure," she replied. "Could you please smell them?"

I was shocked, and it took all my willpower not to burst into tears. It was like the tip of the waterfall, because once you start sliding down that cascade to puberty, there isn't any going back.

And even if Casey retains her innate modesty, there are so many images in the media that are bombarding kids and tweens and teens that you've got to keep your eyes and ears open. I do what I can to make sure Casey and Cole understand what we expect of them. If they act up, there are consequences. They're Parhams, and Parhams try to do the right thing. Parhams do not get pregnant or get others pregnant at fourteen.

Hopefully, I won't mess up the seed spiels to come, because they're coming soon. I sure don't want to trip up, because children need to know they can talk to their moms about anything, no matter how weird or hilarious (as sex can seem to kids, or at least to Cole). My children know I tell them the truth, and that I'm not going to lie to them about something as important as pregnancy and sexually transmitted diseases.

Okay, ignore the fact that I did lie about Santa and the tooth fairy. Somehow, they're not quite on the same level as chlamydia.

If I ever hesitate about talking about these things, I remember the story a friend of mine relayed as a warning to keep the "talk" flowing, because she knows she blew it.

"My daughter walked in on my husband," she told me, "when he was parading around our bedroom in the buff and thought she was downstairs.

"'What was that *thing*?' my daughter asked me.

"'No *thing*, I didn't see ANYTHING!' I stupidly replied.

"She told me she'd seen a *thing*, and I continued to tell her she hadn't. My reasoning was that I didn't know what to say, so I thought if I said nothing, I could be only a little bit wrong. But if I actually said something, I could be *really* wrong."

So when it's time for the "talk," remember that the embarrassment lasts for only a split second. It, too, shall pass. In the long run, biological imperatives are not going to go flying away with the birds and the bees, and babies will continue to be made the way they've always been made. But how your kids find out about it is entirely up to you.

affluenza season

GOOD-ENOUGH MOTHERS KNOW ALL ABOUT shortcuts. Why, it's practically our middle name!

Shortcuts are especially critical during the tail end of December, otherwise known as Affluenza Season. My shortcut—the one that has saved my sanity for more years than I can count—is that I married a man who loves to do all the holiday cooking.

Too bad he doesn't love to do all the holiday shopping.

I think that all moms, no matter what their faith, struggle with the expectations of Affluenza Season, especially with the rosy Norman-Rockwell-type images of happy families shown in commercials starting at 12:01 a.m. the day after Halloween (didn't it used to be the day after Thanksgiving?). You know the ones—of happy families hugging each other while cooing with delight over the keys to a new car wrapped with a red bow so large a chiropractor needs to be on standby, or jumping with glee over whatever toy will not be on the shelves of your local toy store when you go desperately searching for it on Christmas Eve because moms more savvy than you bought it on eBay two months before.

And if your Affluenza Season obligations translate to long hours of stressful travel for the can't-get-out-of-it visits to family members you wish, deep down, were not related to you, and if the only key you've ever received for the holidays was the one to that powder pink jewelry box with the dancing ballerina you got from Aunt Mabel (the one with the moustache and bad breath) when you were six, affluenza can be a little bit tricky to cure.

I decided that the Parhams would have their own traditions, as a sort of family vaccination against affluenza. I've fine-tuned these over the years, and you might find some (or all!) of them helpful. (Feel free to take what you like and discard the rest, like used wrapping paper.)

Tradition number one is to buy a shopping cart full of batteries. However many batteries you *think* you'll need, quadruple it.

Tradition number two is to explain to Casey and Cole that, as Christians, the purpose of Christmas is to celebrate the birthday of Jesus. We bake a cake and sing happy birthday and go to church and are happy.

Well, that's the way it was when they were little. At some point a few years ago we forgot the birthday candles—Christmas became a day that was all about the presents. Buff and I stupidly got carried away, and had such an obscene pile of gifts (from us and from loved ones) stashed under the tree that we looked at each other and felt sick. How could we impress the true meaning of Christmas upon Casey and Cole when they were nearly sick with giddiness at the sight of all those gifts?

Actually, I'm thrilled that the obscene pile happened, because it hasn't happened since. Now we have a Christmas rule that everybody gets four gifts, and that's it, which certainly helps with the next item on the list. . . .

Tradition number three is to explain the difference between "want" and "need." I use many opportunities during the year to impress upon Casey and Cole that there are many kids out there who actually need things, and who don't get fun presents like toys—they don't get *anything*. And I impress upon them that the spirit of the holiday is the spirit of giving.

Fortunately, Casey and Cole's school and church do a pretty good job of donating clothes and unopened toys to the needy. And I let both of them have their wish lists. Wishes are free; toys are not. I make it clear to my kids that they may or may not get what is on that list, and it isn't a negotiable point. If they're not happy about it, then there's always the list for their birthday.

Tradition number four is to take the photos for the holiday cards. If you're like me, you've forgotten to do this when you should have (like in August), so you rush around like a crazy fool to find a photographer who can deliver on time.

Really, I'm not kidding about August. You've got to be prepared for any photographic emergency. See, several years ago we hired a really nice photographer who took some fabulous shots of all of us (Casey was smiling, Cole wasn't mugging too terribly). When he sent the proofs, I picked out the one I liked best and called his studio to place the order.

Only to find out that the really nice photographer had died suddenly. A month before Christmas.

I felt terrible for him and his family, but I also (selfishly) felt pretty bad for me, as Kinko's told me to take a hike when I rushed in there to see if they could make copies of the proofs, which were (justifiably) copyright protected.

So I dragged the Parhams, the whole lot of them, out into the snow, freezing one and all, and after a comical photo session using a camera with a timer, we got a perfectly suitable shot. And yes, Cole was mugging!

Tradition number five is to find a good tree. As a kid we would get a small needle-dropping tree from the grocery store down the street. Years later my mom got an artificial tree, so I got used to having a non-needle-dropping fake in the living room in Dallas. In fact, our tree lasted for more than ten years. Every year I'd haul it out of the basement, shake the dust off, and admire its silver, uh, sheen, although the wear and tear left it a tad scrawny.

Well, when we moved to the town we refer to as Picketfenceville, I told Buff that it would be a bit obscene to have a denuded plastic silver tree in the house, especially when we live in these beautiful surroundings where there are gorgeous huge tress covered with snow visible right outside our picture windows.

So now we have a pungent and delicious fresh firetrap in our house each year.

Tradition number six is to delegate the decoration of the tree. A couple of years ago I got carried away with the hanging of the ornaments. Casey and Cole wanted to help, but I told them that they didn't know what they were doing, that the little orbs were really fragile, and the ornaments had to hang just so. Disappointed, the kids trudged upstairs to play video games while I arranged the ornaments in perfect order, until half of them fell off and shattered into fine shards that took about three hours to vacuum up.

Served me right! A good-enough mother doesn't need to have ornaments hanging in perfect symmetry. I'm okay with them looking haphazard and sloppy and droopy. In fact, I'm more than okay with however our tree looks, as long as Casey and Cole have fun decorating it while I mock-direct from the comfort of the sofa. Besides, they have a lot more fun decorating than I ever did, and I have a blast watching them.

And to spare the worry about how nice and neat the decorations are on the outside of the house, I got an enormous Frosty the Snowman that blows up to be about eight feet tall. He stands next to the tacky light-up reindeer, and if I'm really lucky this year, they'll both topple over during a blizzard and next year we'll make do with a simple wreath on the door.

Tradition number seven is to let the kids open one gift on Christmas Eve. This is a tradition started by my parents, who always got to choose the gaily wrapped box for my sister and me.

Every year, we got excited. Every year we were crushed, because Mom and Dad's Christmas Eve gift of choice was inevitably *pajamas*, so we'd look all cute and adorable in the photos that would be taken in the morning. Mom and Dad would coo and gush, and Tracy and I would look at each other and grit our teeth and say, "Gee, thanks," even though we sure didn't mean it.

In my world, pajamas don't count as a gift. Pajamas count as torture.

I suggest allowing the kids to choose one present, and keep the boxes with the pajamas stashed in the closet till the morning!

Tradition number eight is to go online to www.noradsanta.org on Christmas Eve, where you can track Santa's progress in the air.

I figure I'm probably in the minority of Christmas-celebrating moms who has kids still believing in Santa at the advanced ages of eight and ten. It'll be tough for them when they accept reality for good, although they've been hearing for years from their more jaded or non-Christian classmates that Santa doesn't exist (and that's fair enough!). Once Casey deals with the truth, no way will she be able to keep it secret from Cole.

When the kids have come home crying that the other kids don't believe that Santa is real, I've told them that it's okay because we believe. I explain that some kids have a faith that is different from ours, and they don't celebrate Christmas, and their beliefs are as important to them as ours are to us. I figure that this is an important enough lesson, and that perhaps my kids will forgive me for stringing the Santa myth out as long as I have. They'll probably forgive me about thirty years from now, when they have kids of their own and don't want to break their bubble of Santa love.

Tradition number nine is to be realistic for Christmas Day itself. Plan to be awakened during the darkest hours just before dawn (if you haven't already been up all night searching for D batteries that you can't find because you forgot all about tradition number one). Then, as soon as the gifts are opened and gushed over and broken, eat some breakfast, down a mimosa, and crawl back into bed. Works for me!

Tradition number ten is to try to make Affluenza Season about each other, not about stuff or unrealistic expectations. Every year I see countless moms walking down the street with their shoulders hunched up around their ears, looking as if they're carrying the weight of the world. I'd like to give them all a gift this Affluenza Season, the gift of cutting themselves some slack.

This year try to create your own non-Norman-Rockwell-type picture of what you'd like to see most for the holidays, and carry that around in your mind instead. If that means you don't get *all* the decorations up this year, fine; if you can't find the hand-painted dreidel the Dreaded Super-Mom said was a must-buy, fine; if you can't find the Kwanzaa kinara after driving around like a maniac and going to fourteen stores before lucking upon T.J. Maxx, which is where I found the one that Cole had been asking about, *fine*!

Better yet, I try to hang with my kids whenever I can. And when you do hang out together, you should hopefully be enjoying the true meaning of holiday spirit. No, not the spirit accompanying the "Mom, he's playing with my toy!" "Mom, she's making fun of me!" "Mom, he kicked me!" "Mom, I'm bored!" "Mom, I'm cold!" "Mom, why did Jeremy get a Power Rangers Megazord and I didn't?" emanating from your kids' mouths.

The kind of holiday spirit I find in a bottle of Châteauneuf du Pape, vintage 1988. A good year. A very good year indeed.

never put unleaded
gas in a diesel car

OUR LIVES ARE SO FULL—FULL OF SCHOOLWORK
and homework for the kids, and stressful work for adults—that
vacations are a must-have. I know lots of other families who
don't schedule regular trips, but I sure don't understand that.
I'm taking every damn vacation I can get!

On one of our annual jaunts, Buff and I were both in dire
need of couple-time. I mean, if you ignore the primary relationship in your life, the secondary relationships are all going to
suffer, right? Buff and I needed to spend time alone together, to
get away from the daily demands, and maybe even remember
what it was like to turn off the lights and not go right to sleep.

So we dumped the kids with my mom (who was thrilled to
have them to herself), and off we flew to Paris for a few days,
where neither of us had ever been. Buff wasn't worried about
that pesky they-speak-French-in-France issue, as he'd gotten
all A's in his high school French class, although he'd conve-
niently forgotten that he'd graduated some thirty-odd years
ago and hadn't conjugated a verb since.

Well, the first morning there, my curling iron broke, which
for this black woman was pretty high on my list of possible

catastrophes. After wasting practically an entire day in search of a replacement, I gave up, and realized it was the best thing to have happened: I was liberated from that annoying hour in the bathroom every day, and I had one less thing to worry about. Plus, I now had a perfect excuse to run out and buy a lot of gorgeous French silk scarves, to tie over what was soon to be a head of very unruly locks.

Then we decided to drive to Normandy, planning to stop on the way to see Monet's gardens before arriving at the American cemetery. But we naively broke the first rule of international travel before we even left town. We split up to go shopping—with no cell phones or other means of reaching each other. Several hours later I was a whirling dervish of frustrated relief when we finally found each other again, and once I stopped screaming at Buff, we got into the rented Yugo and drove north.

All the angry glares and recriminations we were giving each other made us ravenous, so after driving for a while, we pulled into a truck stop for lunch. I glanced around and noticed all the French truckers gaily consuming vast carafes of wine and then getting back on the road. I remember thinking this could not be good, but when we were served some of the best food (and wine) I've ever consumed, all was forgiven.

When we finally got going again, Buff broke the second rule of international travel, which was to ask the locals in his unintelligible French for directions. When we realized a while later that we were hopelessly lost, we drove to a village, found a drugstore that was miraculously still open, bought two toothbrushes and some toothpaste, and ended up spending the night at a converted monastery.

Off we went to our cell. We sat down on the thin mattress,

looked at each other, and burst into uncontrollable laughter. Getting lost turned out to be the best thing that had ever happened to us on vacation. We weren't going to make it to our destination when we thought we would, but so what? We actually didn't have an agenda; we weren't stuck with any group— so why were we going crazy, racing up the autoroute to see the cemetery before dark? It would still be there in the morning.

We found it easily the next morning, of course.

But then, on the way back, we mistakenly put unleaded fuel in the car's diesel engine, and Buff was so afraid the car would blow up if we stopped that we basically just threw the money for the tolls at the booths and kept on going in a panic. And I was thinking the whole time that the people in the gas station who'd watched us fill this car were snickering to themselves, "Stupid Americans!"

On our last day we were standing in line to get into the Musée d'Orsay when we heard a very long announcement in French.

"What did they say?" I asked Buff.

"They said 'Welcome,'" he replied.

Then they repeated the announcement in English. Yeah, they said welcome all right—welcome and au revoir, since the workers had just gone on strike.

We never did get into the Musée d'Orsay, but we had a pretty carefree time anyway. Sure, my hair looked like a Brillo pad, but we never would have had those adventures if the kids had been there.

I felt like a different person during that trip. I laughed more. I was more adventurous in my eating. Yep, health-conscious, spin-class-obsessive *moi* ate tons of things I normally wouldn't, such as chocolate croissants for breakfast (much more delicious than my usual health-food-store cereal and soy milk) and Monte Cristos, which are basically deep-fried cholesterol sandwiches. (How is it that the French are not falling down dead in the streets from heart disease?)

Then I discovered how delicious a Kir is, particularly when you have one for lunch, teatime, and dinner.

More important, I fell in love with Buff all over again. Sure, I knew that you have to have vacations away from the kids in order to stay sane as a person, but you also need to rekindle your relationship with your partner in life. Not all necessary vacations are *family* vacations. It's much easier to have intimate, extended conversations when you aren't interrupted by "He's hitting me!" every five minutes, and, instead, can look back over your life together, marveling at the changes and planning for the future.

I also learned that the best vacations can be those where you allow yourself to be spontaneous, and get out of the rut of your comfort zone.

As long as I remember to never again put unleaded gas in a diesel car.

pray for forgiveness

"WAS JESUS EVER A TEENAGER?" COLE ONCE ASKED.

"Of course he was," I told him.

"Did he do normal teenage things?"

"Like what?"

"Like hang out with hot chicks?"

Yeah, baby—hot biblical chicks!

Having a spiritual life is very important to me and to Buff. I was raised as a nondenominational Christian, and my family went to church every week. I loved it. Buff loved his church too. So instilling our beliefs in our children is an integral part of our lives. I want them to understand what we believe and why we believe what we do, so that when they go out into the world and see other belief systems, they'll have a firm basis in their own religion while remaining open to learning about how others pray too.

And for us, church—or synagogue, or mosque, or temple—isn't just about prayer. It's about being a part of a community, and about giving back. It's about establishing yourself as a thinking, feeling, spiritual being with a place in the world.

The thing with church and children is that the church

building itself can't be too far away. You don't need to hear one more excuse about why not to go on chilly Sunday mornings when you're trying to drag your charming offspring out of bed.

Kids have to be entertained as well as informed. It's easier to drag the little monsters out of bed when they know they'll be seeing their church friends a short while later. At our church Casey and Cole stay with us in the service for about half an hour, which kills them because there's a lot of emotional singing, and then they quickly run off to Sunday school, where parents are mercifully told to let them have their lessons in peace.

The church we go to now has its roots in the Pentecostal faith, and the congregants there are very demonstrative in their worship. It took me a while to get used to services. In fact, the first time we went there, I noticed that everyone was sort of muttering under their breath, and I thought, *Why is everyone talking? Don't they realize that we're praying here?*

One time at services a woman was praying with me in the aisle after we had been dismissed. And there was my charming Cole, trying to get my attention by tapping on my bowed head! "Stop it!" I hissed, loudly, and not just once, until he finally got bored and went to find Casey.

Fast-forward a few months to a time when I walked into the foyer and someone asked me if I was Cole's mom. I said yes, thinking she was going to say something sweet about my little boy.

"Do you think you can talk to him before he comes to church? Because he is kind of rambunctious," she said instead.

"We have a really good group of kids that come here, and he is *very* distracting."

My heart fell down to my shiny red toes. *Omigod*, I thought, *my kid is going to hell. And not only is he going—but he's also bringing the other kids with him!*

It's hard to know how much of the spirituality part of churchgoing sinks in with the kids. As with so many other lessons in parenthood, all you can do is plant the seed—then hope for the best.

Which leads to some memorable conversations at home. Both Cole and Casey have at one point or another been preoccupied with the concept of what happens when you die. It took quite a while for them to understand the notion of a soul and to understand that when your body goes into the ground at your funeral, your essence is no longer there. It was a bit easier for them to digest this once they realized that heaven was a very, very nice place, where they could have all the toys they wanted, and the batteries would never run out of juice.

Emmanuel, the son of my cowriter, has the same notion of heaven. Once when he was about three, he got very upset about something, so Karen asked him what was wrong.

"Mommy, I said a bad word yesterday," he eventually confessed. "Does that mean I am going to hell?"

"No," she replied, smiling sweetly. "You are not judged on things like that. God's ability to forgive is much greater than mine."

Especially once she found out he'd said that bad word in front of his preschool teacher.

the untimely demise of night-nite bear

WE ALL NEED OUR COMFORT OBJECTS.

When Cole was born, he was given a very special baby gift: an exceptionally ugly bear dressed up in a rabbit suit. Goofy, sure, but this bear quickly became extra special to Cole, who loved to chew on the bear's nose. For the first seven hundred days of his life, Cole was never seen without the creature we dubbed Night-Nite Bear.

During one catastrophic night when Cole was about two-and-a-half, he left Night-Nite Bear outside. Well, the elements finally did to Night-Nite Bear's nose (and the rest of him) what Cole had been attempting to do for months, and when we found Night-Nite Bear in the morning, he was even more bedraggled than usual, with a nose that flopped right over. Cole was very concerned, and then became increasingly upset. So I took the bear to the seamstress up the street, where he underwent an emergency rhinoplasty and became nearly as good as new (considering what a mess he'd already been!).

As Cole became more attached to Night-Nite Bear and hauled that thing with him everywhere, I began having night-mares and panic attacks that the bear might accidentally be left in the church nursery or at a restaurant. In an effort to head trouble off at the pass, I searched the Internet for a back-up Night-Nite, but to no avail. Then I asked the woman who'd given Night-Nite Bear to Cole as a baby gift, but she couldn't remember where she'd gotten him.

I expect you know what's coming next.

One year, feeling brave and proud of my mommy progress, I (stupidly) decided to take the kids on our annual trek to kid mecca, aka Orlando, Florida, by myself.

Okay, what's wrong with *that* picture?

In my quest to make our vacation not only good enough but also *better* than good enough, I (stupidly) rented a convertible. I should have known this was ill-fated, and not just because I wasn't heeding my own advice about having this vacation—and all other vacations—be good enough, *not* perfect. No, I really should have known I was in trouble when Cole, who was at the age when potties were still (literally) hit or miss, peed all over the Hertz counter.

Undeterred by that momentary setback, we hopped into the convertible and headed east to the time-share. I was strapped in; the kids were strapped into their car seats. Night-Nite Bear was not. He was (stupidly) in the hands of a carefree toddler.

The sun was shining, the music was blasting, I was traveling a good ten miles per hour *under* the speed limit, and we were feeling sensationally happy as the sun beat down on our faces and the wind tossed our hair into great mountains of frizz.

But in an instant, tragedy struck. And it was totally my fault, because I saw it coming.

I happened to be peering into the rearview mirror in time to see Cole throwing Night-Nite Bear up in the air again and again. Just as the words "Cole, Night-Nite Bear is going to go bye-bye if you keep" came out of my mouth—whoosh! Out of Cole's hands, down the trunk, and onto the road flew the exceptionally ugly bear dressed in a rabbit suit. For once Night-Nite Bear actually seemed a thing of grace, soaring out of the car like an eagle.

I had a decision to make in that split second, and as hard as it was, I believe to this day that I made the right one. I could have stopped the car on the side of the road and looked for Night-Nite Bear, and risked harm to my happy family for a fifteen-dollar stuffed bear, or I could have promised Cole we'd find an even better Night-Nite Bear . . . one that would be better, faster, and stronger than the old Night-Nite Bear.

Which is exactly what I did, before we even got to the time-share. . . . Do not pass go, do not collect two hundred dollars, go right to FAO Schwarz. With that panicked look that only parents in trouble wear like a badge of dishonor on their faces, I tore into the store, looking for a suitable replacement, because I'm sure you understand what a big, hairy deal losing Night-Nite Bear was. So there we were, three knuckleheads squeezing and tugging all the bears in the newborn section, until we found one that was just right enough to stop Cole's sobbing. Since there could only ever be one Night-Nite Bear, this bear was promptly dubbed Night-Nite Two.

Night-Nite Two served us well, although he was never quite as comforting to Cole as the original. But don't think for a minute that every time I drive west on 408 in Orlando, every single year for the past seven years, I don't crane my neck on that stretch of road, hoping against all hope to find Night-Nite Bear.

We all take our comfort wherever we can find it!

And I would highly recommend buying duplicates if not triplicates of your child's favorite loveys. The replacements won't have the same smell (okay, *stench*, despite repeated washings) or chewed-off fingers or stains on the butt, but they'll help many of our little ones fall asleep and give us a moment's peace!

As kids grow older, their need for comfort objects evolves. Some kids like to carry a lucky penny or a dangling charm in their backpacks; others like to rub on a square cut from their old blankie before it disintegrated entirely. And some kids find comfort in stories. Karen's son, Emmanuel, is a particular fan of stories about the time she cracked her chin open and needed stitches, or when Kelly the dog chased a porcupine and got a face full of quills (something I can relate to, having watched Olivia in action). I think that hearing about the disasters their moms survived when young helps children visualize us as little people who were once as needy of protection as they are now.

Some months ago Casey was gearing up for a very important test. I could tell she was nervous about it because it was all she could talk about for weeks. One night, when Cole had already gone to bed, I sat her down for a cuddle and told her all about my own heinous school experiences, and how I sometimes still get nervous interviewing certain guests. She was astonished that I still suffer from nerves and vulnerability, even when I don't show it on TV.

"Is it stressful being a grown-up?" she asked.

"It sure is," I told her. "It's just that adults have a different kind of stress than kids do. But we all want to do good work, and make people proud, and stay healthy."

Then I showed her some breathing techniques, but I could tell her anxiety level was still way up there, and that our pep talk had run out of fizz. She remained a wreck during the week leading up to the exam.

I knew I would already be at work when she'd be leaving for school on test day, so I came up with the next best thing. I wrote a note and attached it to her folder with three colored paper clips, explaining that if she took the paper clips with her, she could remember the things I'd taught her about the test (and breathing deeply) and it would almost be like I was there with her.

That afternoon Casey told me those paper clips made all the difference in the world, and she was sure she'd aced the test.

My kids aren't the only ones who need a comfort object from time to time. When I need comfort, there's one infallible source for me.

No, not Buff. A glass of wine from the bottle of Bordeaux that Buff bought me.

At the end of a very long day, it's not just the red wine I savor—it's the ritual of filling up my special glass with precisely four ounces, dumping enough scented cream into the tub to grease a moose, lighting more than a few candles and praying I don't set off the fire alarm, and pouring myself into a long, hot, soaking bath.

Now if only I could relax in there for more than five minutes before the choir tunes up with the "Mom, I need you!" chorus.

when mom's away,
the cat will play

I WAS OFF ON ASSIGNMENT WHILE BUFF WAS holding down the fort at home, and I had just spent some welcomed downtime in Canton, Texas, at my most favorite flea market in the whole wide world. Ever since my first trip there ages ago, when I spent five hundred dollars on crap (as Buff calls it) I couldn't then afford, I've gotten a kick out of unearthing whatever crap people are happy to sell to the deluded such as myself.

I just love flea markets. They're the outdoor equivalent of a sale at Target or T.J. Maxx.

Anyway, I was enjoying the incredible high of paying top dollar for a carload of more crap when my phone rang. I turned down Journey (guilty pleasure, no critics need comment, thank you very much), which was blaring on the radio, and picked up my phone, only to hear what sounded like an ox being disemboweled.

Casey was crying and carrying on, and in the background all I could hear was Buff yelling at her to calm down. Yeah, that's effective!

Needless to say this phone call was a total buzz kill.

And all because of a tooth. It seemed that one molar had announced its intention of leaving her mouth a few weeks before, so she'd gotten used to the weeks of familiar wobbling with each chew. Suddenly another molar had the audacity to surprise Casey and fall out quite unexpectedly, while she'd been enjoying a piece of her favorite sticky candy.

"Mommy," Casey said in between hiccups and sobs, "how many molars do I still have?"

A quick mental check of what I'd retained from the dozens of baby books I'd read over the years came up empty. "I think you have eight all together," I guessed, wishing the number were more like two. "And all your other teeth."

Immediately came more wringing of hands and gnashing of teeth between her sobs. "Oh no, I don't want to go through this six more times."

I didn't have the heart to tell her at that moment that *all* her baby teeth would fall out, as my own heart was full to bursting. It's moments like those—the inability to be there when your child needs you—that make being a working mother, whose job takes her on the road, tough. Buff is a wonderful dad and a loving presence when I'm away, but sometimes only Mom will do.

With a deep sigh I hung up the phone, determined to let Buff focus all his attention on the issue at hand, because Lord knows, men are not blessed with the multitasking gene. Heck, I'm the woman who could answer the door while nursing Cole, with Casey attached to one leg, sign for the UPS package, and light the deliveryman's cigarette all at the same time.

When Mom's away and Dad's in charge, you're just going to have to bite the bullet and admit that it ain't going to be done the way you want it done. The bed might not be made; hair might not be combed; the kids will be scarfing down McDonald's for breakfast, lunch, and dinner while the organic carrots are left to rot. But the kids will be safe and fine without you. It'll be good enough, sure, but it won't be *your* good enough.

That's hard for me. I think it's hard for most moms, whether they depend on a husband or partner or babysitter to do the essential caretaking in their absence.

What's especially hard for me to deal with is my as-yet-unfulfilled wish that Buff would interact more with the kids when I'm away. Instead, Casey and Cole are invariably upstairs on the computer or watching TV, while he's downstairs watching ESPN.

That's Buff's version of togetherness.

"Whaddaya mean we're not together?" Buff wants to know when I call him out on this. "They're in the same house, aren't they?"

See, I know he doesn't quite get, in his gut, how important it is for me to just *be* with the kids. This doesn't necessarily mean we have to do anything or go anywhere special. I can remember when the kids were small and I'd tell Buff I needed him to watch the kids, and he'd reply that he had to do the dishes. I'd explain yet again that he didn't have to *watch* them every second, but he just had to have them with him. We had a completely different mind-set about what togetherness meant.

When I get home from work, I have a visceral, physiological need to be with Casey and Cole. I've been apart from them all day, and yet in ten minutes they'll say, "Okay, we told you how our day was. Now you've got to let us go play. We need space."

When Buff gets home from work, the first thing he says is "See you later," and then he goes into his study to decompress. The ESPN is turned on and the kids are turned off.

To be fair, Buff's parenting style is his own. Our children have two different parents and we approach parenting from very different angles, which actually isn't such a bad thing. I've got to let Buff figure out his own way with the kids. Nor does he mind being in charge when I'm away, since they get a big kick out of planning special fun things to do together. Casey and Cole both know he loves them dearly.

Plus, I know that when I come home, no one will have gone to the emergency room. For me, it's a good lesson in not sweating the small stuff.

But the small stuff is still what I have to deal with when I'm out of town. The kids will call me about sorting out playdates or to talk about their teachers, or to just hear my voice. For our family there are certain things that Mommy just has to do, no matter where she is.

So I often feel that I'm never really away, or fully disengaged. I could be on the far side of the moon and I'd still have one foot stuck on the Parham estate.

Take, for instance, the time I was on a business trip in Maui (seriously!) and Buff was in charge at home. Every time I called him, which wasn't easy, seeing as there was a six-hour time difference, he would tell me that all was under control. He even took it a step further.

"I really love this Mr. Mom thing," he proudly declared.

The afternoon before I was due to come home, I felt a

little, teeny scratch in my throat. Well, multiply that by no sleep and flying for ten hours at thirty-nine thousand feet, and that little scratch had blossomed into a full-blown cold by the time I landed the following morning.

But of course, there was no time to stay home and get the deep sleep I needed, with the door shut, the phone off, and the earplugs in. Oh, no. Casey had a birthday party to go to at a local indoor baseball facility, which gave Cole the great idea that he, too, wanted to take some at-bats.

Chump that I am, I dragged myself all over upstate New York looking for someplace, any place, that had batting cages. Finally found them. Screamed in joy at Cole each time he hit the ball. Picked up Casey and, utterly exhausted, managed to get home, tuck in the kids, and pour my germ-laden self into the bed.

A few hours later Cole shook me awake, telling me that he, too, was sick. Crap. So I made an end-of day appointment for him at the doctor's, hauled my carcass out of bed, and took him there. Where I blew my nose and wiped my bleary eyes and finally got a good look at my son's face.

And idly wondered why my son looked like one of those angry cartoon characters. You know, the ones whose brows are permanently furrowed?

After peering at him more closely, it dawned on me. Cole looked like that because the ends of his eyebrows were *gone*! Where, precisely, had they gone *to*? And *how*?

"Cole, what the hell happened to your eyebrows?" I asked.

He shrugged his shoulders, slightly embarrassed by the nature of my questioning, so I whipped out the BlackBerry and e-mailed Buff.

You're not gonna believe this, began the e-mail.

His response? *Oh yeah, while you were in Hawaii, I knew there was something I forgot to tell you.*

He may have enjoyed his Mr. Mom moment, but next time I go out of town, I'm taking every razor I own with me.

every day is mother's day

"MOMMY, I NEED TO TALK TO YOU!" CASEY said, rapping on the door.

"I'll be out in a minute," I replied.

"No, really, I need to talk to you right away!" Casey retorted, her voice dripping with urgency. Then she opened the door.

Never mind that I was sitting in the bathroom, tweezing my eyebrows and shaving my legs.

She looked at me and smiled winningly, her dimples flashing. I am happy to report that I did not smile back. Instead, I said, "Excuse me, just what the heck do you think you're doing in here? I NEED MY PRIVACY!"

Then I shooed her out as best I could, and she got the message.

Casey didn't really need to talk to me at that moment, of course. She just *felt* like talking. But I need time in the bathroom, for crying out loud! And she needs to respect my boundaries, my privacy, and my need to do some things on my own. Whether it's something simple, like, oh, I don't know, tweezing my brows, or something more complicated, like getting the hell out of Dodge.

After all, sometimes the demands on me seem to be so, well, *demanding* that I find myself close to teetering on the precipice. Were I to slip or slide into the great abyss, I know one last, sweetly comforting thought would flash though my mind: *At least I'm alone and nobody knows where to find me!*

This concept isn't just about my needing time apart from Casey and Cole to do my own thing. A good-enough mother knows that her children need to be away from *her*, too.

Yet this simple concept is anathema to a vast horde of other moms out there. They're under so much social pressure and peer pressure and partner pressure that they start to believe the "Mommy is no longer allowed to have a life" myth. The myth that tells all of us that once you become a mother, you're suddenly obliged to put aside every single aspect of what makes you, *you*.

What's *that* all about? Are you not a good-enough mother if you want to have a few hours every once in a while (or, God forbid, a whole day!) all to yourself, to dream about what you want to dream about, or to even try to do what you dream about? I mean, when you're sitting on an airplane and the video starts playing with the instructions about what to do in an emergency, what do they tell you you're supposed to do with the oxygen masks? Put one on your own face before you put one on your child's. You have to take care of yourself before you take care of others. Why is that perceived as selfish?

And while I'm on the subject, how can you talk about raising children to be free-thinking, independent, fully functioning members of society, with their own ideas and the confidence to follow them on the path of their own choosing, if you're not doing this yourself? Do you really want to be a helicopter mom, hovering over your kids to make everything all better, when in truth you can't truly do anything of the sort?

Wanting to shelter your kids from the harsh realities of the world is one thing; raising them in a bubble so that they have no skills to cope on their own is another.

Raising kids who can't make decisions on their own or who expect to be rescued because Mommy and Daddy are always covering their butts for them is not going to create capable kids who can live through—and triumph over—the tough stuff.

I do not want children who flip out when they get to college and realize they have to do their own laundry and write their own papers. Enfeebling my child's budding sense of self is definitely *not* good enough for me. Instead, when Casey and Cole do leave the Parham estate, when Buff and I lower the drawbridge and they ride off on their white horses over the moat, I want Casey and Cole to be armed with weapons to tackle whatever wild creatures come their way.

For me, good-enough mothering is about unconditional love, but it's also about unconditional trust. Casey and Cole know I trust them to do the right thing, and that I'll give them the chance to do the right thing. If they don't do the right thing, they know I will not judge them, and I'll do my utmost to guide them in the right direction. I might be angry; I might make them suffer the consequences of their actions; but they know they can trust me to be fair—as long as they tell me the truth and own up to their behavior.

And the only way to be able to trust your children is if you raise them to trust their own judgment *on their own*. This is where my need to impose strict boundaries for privacy, and my need for space so I can do my own internal work, is paying off.

Getting the kids to follow some form of sleep routine was one of the first parenting decisions that truly involved my kids having to do something on their own. Boy, was I a mess about it. I'd put Casey down and force myself to hurry right outside her door. There I'd sit, hugging my knees to my chest with my own thumb in my mouth, crying, "Oh, my baby, my baby! My baby's crying! My baby needs me! I'm a terrible mother! My baby!"

She had me a lot better trained than I did her.

And when she was old enough to scream "Mommy!" . . . forget it. I was a blubbering ball of mush. No word is more powerful than the "Mommy!" being exhaled by a small pair of nuclear-strength lungs.

By the time Cole popped out, I was so exhausted that I became determined to change tactics. Once he was weaned from the hourly feedings he loved so well, I'd put him down, make sure he was dry, put in the earplugs, walk out the door, close it behind me, and then go into my room and close my door. Surprise! Three days later that baby was sleeping through the night without so much as a peep.

Well, this wasn't just great for my kids, who got enough sleep to fuel whatever havoc they planned to wreak the next day, but it was also a powerful lesson for me—in letting go.

See, I need to recharge my batteries too. I need sleep. I need time with Buff. I need time to do my work. And I need time just to chill.

If I don't get charged up, chances are a lot higher that I'll walk into our pristine (for once) house wearing the grime of my day and take it out on my children. They're still too young to not take it personally, and they absorb the impact of my moodiness without the benefit of psychological air bags. When that happens, they may very well internalize what I've unwittingly dished out. Sometimes it's too easy for grown-ups to forget how potent an impact we have on our children.

I'm always reminded of that when Cole gets a funny look on his face and says, "Mom, are you mad at me?"

Okay, so it's Cole asking, which means my first response is usually, "Why, *should* I be?"

If he says no, however, I realize I've got to lighten up, and pronto.

Or sometimes Casey will be sitting with me and she'll say, "I wish you were home more." Whenever I hear that, I know it's not about my physical presence but about my being fully engaged and emotionally available to her when she needs me. And so I'll put down whatever I'm doing, like nuking a frozen burrito or going through paperwork, and find the time to listen to what she wants to talk about.

But on the whole, we're a pretty good team.

As long as I get my space.

Which is why this last Mother's Day was so infuriating. Work was stressful and Buff needed attention and the kids needed attention, and no one was thinking that maybe René needed a break too.

So when Buff asked me what I wanted for Mother's Day, I told him. I said I wanted my loved ones to LEAVE ME ALONE.

All day. Not part of the day. *All* day.

Okay, so maybe that sounded a little harsh. But any working mom with young children understands the importance of a little time to herself. And it wasn't as if I'd been asking for a huge chunk of time alone every day, or every weekend, or even once a month. It was just one day. One Mother's Day.

Yep, on that Mother's Day, I was determined to be the contrarian. I didn't want the kids gurgling over me. Next year I may feel otherwise. But right then I wanted them out of my hair.

Buff's eyes lit up. "Fine," he said. Doubtless he was thinking that getting out of my hair sure was a lot cheaper than some piece of jewelry.

Finally, after counting down the hours till I would get some blessed silence and me-time, I woke up on Mother's Day. The sun was shining and I had nothing planned, except to lounge around in bed, throw on some sweats and get a long-overdue manicure and pedicure in the morning, maybe browse through some shops in downtown Picketfenceville, come home to sleep some more, eat chocolate (which has no calories if you eat it on Mother's Day)—you get the picture. Buff had already ordered the tickets for a one p.m. show for himself and the kids at our local movie theater, and I couldn't wait for them to go wolf down the popcorn.

And then, at about ten thirty, just when I was about to roll out of bed to go into town, he called up the stairs, "Bye, honey. I'm just going to run out to the grocery store."

What grocery store? Immediately my blood began to boil. "You said you would take them the *whole* day," I yelled back at him. "Not for an hour or two at the movies. THE. WHOLE. DAY."

All I could hear was the sound of silence.

"I can get a lot more done without them," he had the audacity to shout back up to me.

"Oh, really? But that's *not* the deal!" I shouted. "THE

DEAL WAS FOR YOU TO TAKE THEM FOR THE ENTIRE DAY!"

And then I heard the door slam and the car start up. Did he take the kids? No, he did not.

Fuming, I threw off the covers and paced around the room. So much for all my plans. And then I found out what he'd said to the kids before he left.

"Leave your mother alone," he'd said.

Yeah, that always works like a charm. He might as well have put a big target on my back. Casey and Cole kept tiptoeing into my room to see if I was awake or not. Believe me, I was wide awake when I heard Buff try to steal back into the kitchen an hour or so later.

"When are you leaving?" I asked, and Buff at least had the savvy to get flustered at the tone of my voice.

"Uh, right now," he said with alacrity, and off they went.

Starting next year there's going to be a change for Mother's Day. No, I'm not going off to a spa with my girlfriends. I'm not going shopping in town. I'm going off somewhere BY MYSELF. I'll allow Casey and Cole and Buff to call me in the morning, tell me that they love me and miss me, and then I'll throw the phone out the window.

double whammy, or how to lose your breasts and your job in five short weeks

LATE IN THE MORNING ON NOVEMBER 29, 2006, I was in my office going over my schedule with Jahayra, as we do every day. When I opened up my calendar, though, I saw a meeting scheduled for that Friday with Sean McManus, president of both CBS News and CBS Sports.

This was *not* something I'd see on my schedule every week.

No matter what you do for a living, when the big boss schedules an unexpected meeting, your stomach drops. My inner alarm bell started to shriek. *Calm down,* I told myself. There *had* been whispers about changes being made to *The Early Show,* but nothing concrete.

The whispers had had nothing in them to make me quake about losing my job.

"What's the meeting about?" I asked Jahayra, who told me she didn't know. She knew only that they'd initially wanted the meeting to be on Thursday, but I would be out of town shooting a segment about a Christmas tree farm in rural Massachusetts.

The next two days passed in a blur. Wanting to be punctual on Friday, I arrived a few minutes early at the CBS Broadcast Center, across town from the television studio, and killed time buying a cup of coffee. I had to laugh. The meeting had originally been scheduled for eleven thirty, but I'd had to push it back to nine thirty because Cole's class had a field trip and he was counting on me to be one of the classroom mommies.

Steeling myself, I soon pasted on my professional smile and walked into the room, where I immediately saw Sean along with Steve Friedman, the vice president for morning broadcasts. When Sean walked out for a moment, I mouthed to Steve, with whom I'd worked closely over the previous year, "What's going on?" Okay, so perhaps it was a stupid question, because once I'd seen Sean and Steve waiting for me, I'd been fairly certain this wasn't going to be a social visit.

"You'll have to wait until Sean gets back," he told me, avoiding my glance. That's when I knew for sure.

When Sean returned and shut the door, I tried to lift the coffee cup to my lips, but suddenly it seemed to weigh two tons. I hoped against hope they couldn't see my hand shaking.

"This is the part of the job I hate," Sean began. "We're going to go in a different direction. . . ."

The rest of the conversation melted into a blur, but I managed to piece together that the news division of the *Survivor* network was voting me off the island.

Actually, it was a very short meeting. But perception is a funny thing in times of crisis, because everything moves in seriously slow motion. I remained calm, and am thankful that my sense of humor was still intact.

"It's really hard for me to sit here and tell you this," Sean said.

To which I quickly replied, "Not as hard as it is for me to sit here and listen to you tell it."

We shared an uncomfortable laugh, and then I stood and shook Sean's hand. Steve gave me a big hug, and I promised both men I would give the network my all until I walked out the studio door for the very last time. It was only then that my voice cracked and my eyes began to well with tears—but not one of them spilled over. I am extremely proud of that.

Mrs. Henry can make me cry. But my bosses who've just fired me—*no way!*

There were so many thoughts in my head as I left, that I was certain people walking past me could hear them. One of the first thoughts was how difficult it was going to be to put on a happy face and work for the next three weeks, as if I hadn't been fired with no warning, as if I didn't have a care in the world. (Doesn't this fall into the category of cruel and unusual punishment?) I knew it was going to be the toughest thing I'd ever had to do at work. Tough, but not impossible. I am, after all, a professional.

And I've had enough years of good-enough-mother training to know that you can never let anyone see you sweat.

One of the most frustrating things about my predicament was having this devastating bit of information inside me and not being able to do anything with it. Before I could tell anyone outside of my inner circle, the news had to go through all the official channels, and a press release had to be put out to the media, which I knew would cause a stir, as surprise moves in high-profile jobs always do.

Somehow I arrived at the lobby, and said good-bye to the kindly guard who'd let me skate over the years when I'd forgotten my ID badge.

As soon as I climbed inside a cab, I called my best friend

in the whole world, Buff. He was very surprised when I gave him the news. He had, in fact, completely misread the intent of the meeting, and had been confidently reassuring me that there was no way they were going to fire me.

Hey—no one said he was perfect!

Then I called my agent and gave him the bad news. Back at the studio, the building looked different. It *felt* different. In little over an hour, my comfortable work home had become a house where strangers dwelled.

At the office I told two people: Harry Smith, my wonderful coanchor, with whom I've always been close; and Jahayra, my trusty lieutenant. Both of them looked at me in shocked disbelief. It's strange, because I was still not visibly upset or in tears, partly because the news had to remain quiet, at least for the time being. But halfway into my conversation with Harry, he got up from behind his desk and gave me a bear hug.

That's when I lost it. I mean, I really broke down, with that heaving, sobbing sort of crying.

I wasn't angry, just incredibly sad.

I gave Harry another hug, and then hurried into my own office to change. Cole's class was leaving for its field trip, with or without me. Life goes on. Fired or not, I'd already signed on to be one of the class mommies on Cole's field trip, and class mommy I was going to be. No matter what!

During the ride to join Cole's class, my emotions veered wildly. (My driver, mercifully, did not.) At first I had to deal with the sheer, immense shock of what had happened. Obviously, since all of us on *The Early Show* had been told there'd be changes, we'd been expecting something. But I hadn't thought that when the music stopped I'd be the one without a chair.

Then there was this alternating sense of relief because I realized I would soon be spared the three thirty a.m. wake-up calls.

Then, just as quickly, I had to deal with crashing waves of worry about how this overnight change in my job status might translate into a drastic change in lifestyle. I know I can cope with change; I always have. But dealing with sudden changes is often not always so easy for kids who are prone to worrying about the stability in their lives, especially when the rug has suddenly been pulled out from under the feet of one or both of their parents. Plus, kids always want to know the details, especially the "why." At this point there was no good "why" associated with my sudden shift in status.

Before I knew it, we'd arrived a few minutes ahead of the class at a theater where they were going to enjoy a lesson in filmmaking. So there I stood, light rain falling on my head, with no umbrella and no job.

Had I been a smoker, this would have been an ideal time to suck two butts. And a martini, for that matter.

Instead, I got something a whole lot better. When the bus pulled up, Cole was one of the first to bound off. As soon as he saw me, he shrieked "Mommy! Mommy!" and ran over to me, throwing his arms around my waist.

At that moment I knew there was nothing wrong with me and that I would be okay.

That hug, at least for the moment, was all the cure I needed.

I sat in the darkened theater with Cole and his class, and the hour raced by as I kept one eye on the big screen and the other on the little screen of my BlackBerry, which by then was exploding with e-mails from Buff, my agent, and my publicist.

Team Syler, as we dub ourselves, was hard at work. Honestly, I got this warm surge of pride and contentment when I thought of my team. I felt that with all these people believing in me— the most trusted, loving people from the personal and professional aspects of my life—all would work out not just fine but *better* than fine.

I held on to that thought later in the day, when I broke the news to my kids. Cole was sanguine, quickly accepting the news more readily than Casey because he instantly figured out that I'd be home more, at least until I found another job.

"Does this mean you're just going to be an ordinary housewife now?" he asked with a cheeky smile.

I had to explain that being a housewife was never *ordinary*, but that, yes, I would be around more for now. No, I would not be taking cooking classes. Yes, I would be riding his tail more.

Casey was a tougher sell, and I saw her lips quivering. See, I had been doing something that in retrospect was kind of dumb (or at least short-sighted). Close to bedtime, when I'd be trying to prepare the next day's segments for the show, I'd always tell Casey and Cole that if they didn't leave me alone and let me study, I would do a horrible job and get fired and then we would lose the house.

Well, you guessed it.

"Are we going to lose the house?" she asked, with tears standing in her eyes.

Never before had I so deeply regretted using that adult-speak with her. A child of ten should not have to worry about the roof over her head.

I gave her a huge hug, wiped her eyes, and quickly

explained to her and Cole that television is and always has been a tough and volatile business, and that sometimes people are let go unexpectedly.

"Then why do you keep getting jobs in television?" asked Cole in his infinite wisdom.

Still, that weekend was tough. Despite the amazing amount of support I got, I just wanted to curl up in bed and not have to talk to anyone, but we had a number of official events to go to. One of them was a black-tie tribute to actor Will Smith by the Museum of the Moving Image in Manhattan. I borrowed an absolutely gorgeous Carmen Marc Valvo gown and got all dolled up. No one could have known from my bright smile that anything was wrong. While walking down the red carpet and posing for the paparazzi who were shouting my name, I couldn't help thinking, *Wow, this may be one of the last times I'll be doing this.*

And then I thought, *Oh, no, it isn't!* And then I realized, hey, what the heck. I knew I was glowing. I knew I'd never looked better.

As the weeks went on, I realized that being a lame duck was, well, *interesting.* Someone asked me a question about *The Early Show*, and I could only reply, quoting Robert De Niro from *Meet the Parents*, "I am now outside the circle of trust."

As soon as I said that, I realized I was liberated. It's a word Buff had used when he'd first heard the news, and I'd thought he was saying that only to cheer me up. But then it struck me that, yes, I really *was* about to be liberated. And I realized I would now have the time to find a new job that would showcase not only my skills, but also my wacky sense of humor.

This wacky sense of humor has been what has carried me

through this unforeseen blow. It's like a vaccine, protecting me from the ills of life.

I am pleased with the true me. That's not to say this change hasn't been hard. It has been among the hardest things in my life. Sometimes I feel really good and strong, as if I've been handed the opportunity of a lifetime. Other times I feel utterly defeated and demoralized, with my self-esteem hovering somewhere just above the dirt.

And then there's the practical good-enough-mother part of me. The part that realizes these things happen, that there's an ebb and flow to life that's out of my control—just as my children's personalities and interests are—and that this change is somehow meant to be. I haven't had one day of panic, thinking I have to find another job right away just so I can be back on television in a jiffy. I guess that's the difference between the René of thirty-three and the René of forty-three. At thirty-three I would have been beyond devastated if I'd gotten fired. Now I'm much more patient. I'm thrilled to spend more time with my children.

And I will be back in the game, probably sooner than I think.

But then again, I have to confess that there have been times when I've been sitting in my office, a scant eleven minutes before I'm slated to go on the air, thinking, *I want to disappear. I cannot put on my happy face and do this.*

Then I pull it together, and do it. You know why? Because I am a professional who always gives 100 percent. I can hear the words of the original good-enough mother, Anne Syler, ringing in my ears: "The only fair in life is the weather."

Ain't *that* the truth!

Really, sometimes you can think only in clichés when you're living through the "when it rains, it pours"/"when life gives you lemons, make lemonade" time of your life. I'm especially thinking in clichés right now because I'm not only living with the sudden loss of the job I loved, but I am also dealing with the anticipation of another huge event.

I'm about to have my breasts chopped off.

Okay, perhaps "chopped" isn't quite the right word. "Prophylactic mastectomy" certainly has a more elegant ring to it. But whatever you call it, I had decided to make such a radical move months before I found out about being fired, and the surgery had already been scheduled for January 9, 2007.

I reached the conclusion that such a drastic procedure was right for me after four years of worrying coupled with multiple biopsies that left me disfigured and scarred. Ever since I was diagnosed with the hyperplasia with atypia in September 2003, I've had to have a mammogram every year, followed by increasingly painful biopsies, which are then followed by three anxious days of wondering whether I have breast cancer.

It sucks, to put it mildly!

I had *really* been thinking about this prophylactic surgery as they took me in for my biopsy in September 2006 and put me on the table. "Don't cut my nipple," was the last thing I managed to mumble to my surgeon just before finally slipping into blissful drug-induced sleep. I knew my surgeon had successfully performed what's called a nipple-sparing mastectomy, and I thought, *Well, you never know.*

In no way could I have anticipated just how disfiguring and excruciatingly painful my recovery from this biopsy would be. (Note to the squeamish: You might want to skip the rest of this paragraph!) First off, needles are used to place guide wires, so the technicians and surgeon can figure out where the suspicious area is located. Oh, and by the way, before you go under, these needles that carry the guide wires are inserted into your breast *without* an anesthetic! And then afterward, because this was an invasive surgical procedure, there was fluid in the breast that had to be drained once a week. For three dreadful weeks. This meant a long, long needle had to be inserted deep into the breast to aspirate the fluid, and it hurt like hell.

I remember crying like a baby while the technicians inserted the needles. Then after they all left the room, I cried some more. In fact, the morning of that biopsy I couldn't stop crying. I cried when they asked me my name as I was checking in. I cried when the nurse gave me my gown. I cried when they inserted the needles. I cried when they walked me into the operating room. The tears continued to flow as I lay on the table, while my surgeon promised to take good care of me.

After enduring all those needles, I thought, *I've had it! This is it! I cannot and will not live my life this way and go through this again!* But then, much like with childbirth, that terrible, searing pain goes away and you say to yourself, *Oh, come on. It wasn't really that bad, now, was it?*

At least when you go through the pain of childbirth, the result makes all the suffering worthwhile.

Ultimately, my decision to have the prophylactic mastectomy was driven by many factors being stirred together in one big cauldron of breast stew. The first and most important factor was a desire to make a real and substantial dent in my breast cancer risk. Without breasts, not only will I be freed of the need for regular mammograms and biopsies, but I will also instantly lower my breast cancer risk by about 98 percent.

Buff's comment when he heard that was, "Wow, the surgery seems kinda like a no-brainer, doesn't it." But of course it's not—because they're not *his* breasts; they're mine. And because we're talking about lopping off ostensibly healthy breasts.

Well, at least for now they're still healthy.

The second factor in this decision was that, remember, I not only have a mother who survived breast cancer, but my father lived through his own breast cancer as well. This makes oncologists pay attention, as there tends to be a genetic component to male breast cancer.

The third factor was my having been diagnosed, as I mentioned, in September 2004 with hyperplasia with atypia, which is another breast disease that can increase the risk for breast cancer. This meant that the increasingly unbearable yet mandatory biopsies could be a necessity every year, in perpetuity.

The final, deciding factor came several weeks after my last biopsy. After the breast had been excruciatingly aspirated for three weeks and the swelling had gone down, I was horrified by what remained of my left breast. It was perhaps a half-cup-size smaller than the right breast, with a huge scar to boot. My left breast had literally collapsed on itself.

I couldn't even stand to look at myself in the mirror. We may take them for granted or stuff them into bras that don't quite fit, but breasts are such a huge component of who we are as women. Even with all the trouble they'd given me of late, I liked my breasts. They'd fed my babies. They'd made me feel sexual. They were an integral part of my body.

I felt cheated. I led a healthy life, kept my weight in check, didn't overeat or drink too much or smoke or go in the sun or have any other self-induced risk factors, and yet here I was with these pesky and no-longer-perky breasts giving me hell.

I stirred the cauldron some more, and then it hit me—Buff may well have been right. Seems like a prophylactic mastectomy could be a no-brainer after all.

As soon as I made the decision, I felt as if a huge weight had been lifted off my chest. (Okay, sorry, can't help myself!) Honestly, I'd been on the fence about undergoing this surgery for so long that it was incredibly refreshing to have at least made a decision.

Once I did, I spoke to many, many women who'd already had the surgery. All of these women were incredibly helpful, compassionate, and willing to show a perfect stranger how splendid their surgically reconstructed breasts looked. Not one of them had any regrets whatsoever.

Still, I know I won't have any more feeling in my breasts, and that's a tough concept to live with. I also spoke to several friends who've had their breasts augmented, and they shared details of how, precisely, I'm likely to feel, which helps ease the normal anxieties. (They told me the chest area feels "heavy" afterward, and that you can hardly move, because the implants are inserted up under the muscles of the chest wall, and that I should be prepared for it to hurt, a lot, at least for several days after the procedure.)

I also spoke at length with a therapist who specializes in treating patients having cancer surgery. I wanted to talk to an impartial party, just to make sure I'd covered all my bases and looked at every angle. She assured me I had, and I found myself pleased and comforted that I'd made the right decision—for me.

Sure, I wonder what I'll feel like once I've recuperated from the surgery itself, when there's no way to undo what has been done.

Other than that, I have no real hesitation or trepidation because the pros so grossly outweigh the cons in my mind. Of course there will be armchair critics who might think my decision was way too drastic, but my answer to that is: This is something I need to do for my own health and for my family. I plan to be a good-enough mother for a very long time, thank you very much. And part of being good enough is taking a proactive stance. I'd rather play offense than defense.

So, there you have it. When all of this with my job and my health was going down, I have to admit I spent an inordinate amount of time wondering about life's challenges. You know, the really gritty keep-you-awake-at-night ones—and why they always seem to happen at once. And I've got to say, well, yeah, so they happen at once. I can deal—even while telling myself that it's not fair. Unlike in those mercifully long-gone days in Mr. McCullough's math class, no amount of cramming will help me through some of life's exams.

But I'm going to pass them nonetheless.

epilogue: pajama time

SO NOW YOU KNOW. IN MY CRAZY WORLD, WHERE I'm busy juggling the work/family/everything-else balls high in the sky, I have come to this realization: I am a good-enough mother.

I say this in the way the Reverend Jesse Jackson says, "I *am* somebody."

Yes, I do.

Hear me loud, hear me proud: "I *am* a good-enough mother!"

I figure that anyone who hasn't gotten my message by now just isn't going to get it. And you know me well enough by now to realize all I have to say to these people.

That's right, I Don't Care, because it has just dawned on me that I have to find one hundred objects to hot-glue onto a poster board to commemorate the first one hundred days of school. Dang, we never had to hot-glue anything when I was a kid. We just threw on our designer-label-free clothes and walked to school, safe in the knowledge that Day 100 was pretty much going to be the same as Day 1 and Day 243.

When I was a kid, my mom was always after me to clean

my room. When I was a teenager, forget about it. The screaming matches over the clothes that I left on the floor (big deal,
right? *Wrong*, as far as Mom was concerned) would have
woken grave diggers in the neighboring county. Well, guess
what? The room that was a mess when I was four, fourteen,
and twenty-four is still a mess at forty-four. But my mom was
smart enough to say, okay, fine, be that way—but make sure
that you make enough money to pay someone to clean your
room for you.

What Mom taught me wasn't just about cleanup. What she
did was encourage me to get out there and try everything at
least once. At dinnertime she'd look at the horrified expression
on my face, and say, "All right, I know you don't like liver and
lima beans, but you have to try it." Now, I'd rather have my
eyes poked out with a toothpick than eat liver, but I took one
feeble bite to please her. And to get it over with. And to know
that I could do things I didn't want to, because someone else
whose judgment I trusted said it was good for me.

Mom was also quite adept at handling whatever life threw
at her, especially disappointments. She showed me how to recognize your disappointment, digest it, and deal with it, to work
through it and move on. As a result, I have always been and
always will be a big believer in the idea that failure and disappointment can be fantastic teachers. (Not as good as Mrs.
Henry, perhaps, but up there on the list!)

Because Mom gave me the confidence that I *was* capable
of dealing with disappointment, I also grew to learn that fears
could be confronted and conquered, and that there wasn't
anything that I couldn't accomplish if I really, really wanted
it, and really, really put my mind to it. If I'd wanted to be a

doctor, I could have done it, excepting perhaps the math part—but on the other hand, I have to admit that even my aversion to math could probably be conquered if I chose to conquer it. (Trust me—I *don't* choose to!)

My mom gave me the greatest gift a parent can bestow: the gift of unconditional love. As a result, I learned how to trust myself, and how to be true to myself at the same time.

I'm doing the best I can to raise my children the same way, to give them a home where they can feel safe, surrounded by love. "Home is where the heart is" isn't just a saying—for Buff and me, home is our haven from the big, bad whatever out there.

I mean, hello, we're all learning here! That's what I tell myself as I peer down into the moat that's suddenly full of hungry alligators. It'll be just my luck that I'll have done ninety-nine-and-a-half things right, and the one half of one thing wrong will be the thing that'll let the alligators bite me right on the butt.

I remember when Casey was born and the nurse plopped this beautiful, beautiful baby with Betty Boop lips and masses of straight black hair into my arms, and I took one look and thought, *Hey, wait a minute, this wasn't supposed to happen. Why did God give me a girl? How am I going to handle a girl? What if she doesn't want to clean her room?*

And Cole, well, I'd love to let this boy of mine run like a wild colt, but Buff and I know he's got to be "broken" if he's going to survive. He has to be taught that there are rules in any society. When there's a red light, you stop. When you're old enough to be toilet trained, you don't pee in your pants anymore.

The challenge is to have the wild colts be "broken" without squashing and killing their spirits. For me, the best way to meet that challenge is to raise Casey and Cole by instinct. I'm trusting myself enough to listen to my gut. I just have to believe that I'm going to do the right thing, because it's all I can do.

Instinctively, I *do* know how to be a good-enough mother. I know myself, and through trial and error I've grown to know my kids.

Of course, a good-enough mother knows she'll make errors during the trial!

I also know that Casey and Cole came out of my groaning belly with the foundations of their personalities, and it's my job to let them grow.

When Cole was little, we got into the habit of spending a lot of time in the bed together. What a surprise: Cole still likes to fall asleep lying in the bed next to me. It's home base for him, and for Casey.

That's how secure our bed is. During the workweek our lives are so crammed full of busyness that we often barely get face time with one another. So each night, after whatever one-pot salt-and-MSG-laden meal I've managed to burn for dinner, the kids take their baths and I get my work done for the following day. The kids dry off and put on their pajamas, and gather their books for reading time. Then we all hop into my bed, like three bugs in a rug, and we spend at least thirty minutes reading in silence. Then we get a chance to cuddle and share stories about our day and just generally hang. I find that when we're pajama-clad, the real stuff comes out. We talk about everything, and nothing, and it's a perfect way to end the day.

Pajama time doesn't have to take place in bed. You can make a home base any cozy place in your house. Just think of it as the opposite of a panic room—it's more like an emotional bomb shelter. Set it up on the couch in the den, on pillows strewn across the floor, even on a chair in the laundry room. Anywhere that makes you all feel safe.

I wouldn't trade pajama time for the world. I wish it could last longer. But it can't. Sometimes I wonder how I'll deal with my kids growing too old to want to share pajama time with me, but I'm hopeful that we'll be able to replace it with something else. A more mature way of talking and dealing with Casey and Cole on their level, perhaps.

Wait a minute—who am I kidding? When Cole is twenty years old, he will undoubtedly still be pulling out a whistle and sticking it up his nose to hear what kind of noise it makes when he blows. He'll be the only twenty-year-old I know who goes to bed with a whistle up his nose, but that'll be okay. He'll be *my* twenty-year-old.

And when Cole is twenty, Casey will be twenty-two. I'll be looking at the wonderful young lady she's become, and I hope I'll remember the time she wrote a poem, one that made me bawl my eyes out and one that I'll save forever.

> I am so proud of you
> When I look at a big strong building
> it reminds me of you.
> You make me feel brave.

And that's good enough for me!